T0265614

Zach Williams definitely has a story to tell. As hard as it was for him and those around him during his worst times, his words shine a light on hope and the realization that nothing and no one is ever lost in the eyes and the hands of God. God does work in strange and mysterious ways, and he performed a miracle by transforming Zach into who I believe he is meant to be now. Zach is a great talent and a great inspiration for millions, including me. This is a hard yet wonderful and inspiring read.

DOLLY PARTON

As a fan of his music, as his friend, and as a brother in Christ, I'm proud of my buddy Zach Williams. If his songs have spoken to your heart the way they have mine, then I know his memoir *Rescue Story* is going to be a powerful and inspirational experience for you.

CHRIS PRATT, ACTOR AND PRODUCER

Failure is not final, and our faults don't define us. Zach Williams's new book is a deeply personal telling of his own creation, fall, redemption, and restoration, set to a story and song that will ignite an old church choir singing in your soul, hands raised, reminding you that God does not treat us according to our flawed performance but is forever committed to us because of His unfailing love, demonstrated by the blood of Jesus Christ.

KIRK CAMERON

I need to be surrounded by people who are brave enough to be vulnerable. In these pages, Zach points to his Rescuer and not his own understanding. The humility in this book gives a proud reader like me full permission to need a savior.

WALKER HAYES, MULTI-PLATINUM RECORDING ARTIST

RESCUE STORY

FAITH, FREEDOM, AND FINDING MY WAY HOME

ZACH WILLIAMS

WITH ROBERT NOLAND

ZONDERVAN BOOKS

Rescue Story
Copyright © 2024 by Zachary S. Williams

Published in Grand Rapids, Michigan, by Zondervan. Zondervan is a registered trademark of The Zondervan Corporation, L.L.C., a wholly owned subsidiary of HarperCollins Christian Publishing, Inc.

Requests for information should be addressed to customercare@harpercollins.com.

Zondervan titles may be purchased in bulk for educational, business, fundraising, or sales promotional use. For information, please email SpecialMarkets@Zondervan.com.

ISBN 978-0-310-36846-5 (hardcover)
ISBN 978-0-310-36848-9 (audio)
ISBN 978-0-310-36847-2 (ebook)

Published in association with the literary agency of WTA Media, LLC, Franklin, Tennessee.

Cover design and photography: Micah Kandros
Interior design: Denise Froehlich

Printed in the United States of America

23 24 25 26 27 LBC 5 4 3 2 1

To my wife and children for always standing by my side. To my mom and dad for their constant prayers. And to my family and friends for all the love and support.

There I was empty handed

Crying out from the pit of my despair

There You were in the shadows

Holding out Your hand, You met me there ...

You are my rescue story[1]

CONTENTS

INTRODUCTION
Plan for Me

When I was darkness, You were light
When I was dead You breathed new life
God, You changed my destiny
And now the only thing I see

Your relentless love . . . Ever chasing me[2]

The first night of my 2023 A Hundred Highways Tour was on a drizzly, cool March evening in Columbus, Georgia, at RiverCenter for the Performing Arts. As I sat in my dressing room, I prayed for the strength to follow through on the decision I had made to break the silence on a very personal story, one I had never shared from stage. Up to this point, I had only talked about it with a close circle of family and friends.

In the middle of our set, just before performing the song "Plan for Me," through quite a few tears I had to constantly wipe away with my bandana, along with a broken, repentant heart, as King David wrote in Psalm 51, I shared these words with the sold-out crowd:

"If you have been to one of my concerts before, you've probably heard me talk about how I was raised in church and then, like a lot of kids do, I wandered away from how my parents raised me. I walked away from how I was brought up. Today, I know that my parents are responsible for everything I have in my life. Had it not been for the seeds that they started planting in me from an early age, I wouldn't even be here tonight.

"I worked construction for my dad as he watched me go through my struggle with drugs and alcohol for many years. To be honest with you, I took advantage of Dad's grace. He would do things like pay me, even when, at times, I didn't show up for work. He was always there to share a word of encouragement. With all that was going wrong in my life, I can remember to this day how Dad would say, 'Son, I don't have an answer for you other than Jesus. He's the reason why you're here. He's the reason why your mother and I are still together.'

"I remember when Dad finally told me his own story of life before Jesus. One thing I have come to realize these past few years is the devil comes to attack us with the same things that our parents and our grandparents and their parents struggled with. It's a generational thing.

"Dad told me, 'I'm just like you. I used to struggle with a lot of the same things you did. A while after your mother and I got married, we were on the verge of divorce, much like your own marriage has been. But all that was before we gave our lives to Christ.'

"For me, growing up as a kid, I don't have any memory other than being in church. Because of the relationship my parents had with Jesus, that was the way they brought me up. But I know there were a number of times over the years that they just wanted to throw in the towel and give up on me. They would pray, 'God, what have we done wrong? We've done everything that You've asked us to do, and our son is still living this way.'

"I can remember how my parents used to come to where I was playing and sit sometimes for three hours in a smoky, noisy bar listening to me while I was getting drunk and doing drugs. They would pray for me and try to make sure I got home all right. They also came over to our house to pray for me and my wife."

I could see I was connecting with the audience in Columbus, so I knew the moment had come to go deeper into the specific story Dad had told me. I continued . . .

"What I'm about to tell you, I haven't shared this story publicly, but I figured it was time. When I gave my life to the Lord at thirty-three years old, my dad and I had been working together for about fifteen years. It was a steamy, hot, and humid day in Jonesboro, Arkansas. Inside the dried-in house where we were putting up sheetrock, the air was dead and stagnant. The distinct smell of gypsum and drywall mud hung thick in the air. We had one of those huge squirrel-cage fans that squeaked way too loud with each revolution, but at least offered some movement of air. When Dad decided to break for lunch, we made the call to take our chances outside to try to, hopefully, just maybe, catch some kind of occasional breeze in the shade. Some days we would leave and go eat fast food, with the main reason being to sit in the AC for a half hour and cool off.

"But on this particular day, Dad decided that he and I would stay on the job site. I had no idea he had something he had been waiting so long to share with me and was praying for the right moment. Typically, there would be other subcontractors working on the same house we were, but that day, I don't recall anyone else being there. The only sound was the familiar songs on the radio from the local Christian station that Dad always had playing.

"My father was fifty-nine years old with salt-and-pepper hair and a bit of scruff on his face. Especially in the Arkansas summers, his face and arms became a deep dark brown. He grabbed a sleeve of saltine crackers and a bottle of lemonade, while I got my bag of Funyuns and a Mountain Dew. I remember our main course was splitting a can of Vienna sausages.

"Just after we sat down outside on a stack of sheetrock, Dad put his food down, looked at me, and said, 'Son, I need to tell you something.' He paused as if he was mustering up some strength, then continued. 'Years ago, when you first started playing music, I knew something was different about your decision. You don't just pick up a guitar when you're nineteen and start playing, singing, and writing songs. Then you began playing in bars and started to go down a different path. But your Mom and I just kept trusting and believing that God had a plan for your life.'

"'I've never told you this, but when you were a baby, we had you dedicated to the Lord at church. As we walked down the aisle toward the front, you started screaming and making a lot of noise. The pastor smiled and joked to the congregation, "Man, Zach's got a strong set of lungs on him. Probably going to be a singer someday." After everyone laughed, the pastor's face grew serious, as if he was listening to a voice that no one else could hear.'

"'Zach, he looked at your Mom and I and stated, "This child will be a voice for his generation."'

"Hearing the pastor's words from Dad, after a moment of

feeling speechless, I asked, 'How is it that at thirty-three years old, you've *never* told me this story?'

"He answered, 'Well, I didn't want to put any pressure on you. I didn't want to give you something you had to live up to. But when you started playing music, I knew God's plan was somehow about to start. And now, I believe He has allowed you to walk through all of this to give you a platform to share your story with the world to help so many others.'

"As I reflect back on the pastor's prophecy, I'll be honest with you . . . there are days when I feel undeserving and unworthy of those words. But then I am reminded how God has been using broken people, messed up people, for a long time to do His work . . . so don't let anybody ever tell you that you're not qualified or not worthy to do what God is calling you to do. If He has a plan for *my* life, then He has a plan for *your* life.

"The reason I'm sharing this story is not to point out *anything* about me. I am certainly no 'chosen one.' The word from the pastor has never made me feel special at all. But I want everyone who comes out to hear my songs to know the truth of Jeremiah 29:11: '"For I know the plans I have for you," says the LORD. "They are plans for good and not for disaster, to give you a future and a hope."' That is true for *anyone* who calls upon the name of the Lord—just like I finally discovered at thirty-three years old, after years of trying to outrun my guilt and shame, after straying far from the life I knew I was always supposed to be living."

Taking a deep breath, grateful to get through my first time

of telling this personal story, the band and I went into playing "Plan for Me."

After experiencing the gracious response from the folks gathered that evening in Georgia, I knew I had to keep sharing about that moment with my dad every night I stand on a stage, for as long as the Lord leads me. I know I have a responsibility that comes with that prophecy—to share the truth of Jesus with those who will listen.

Yet on that day when I heard my father speak those words for the first time, spoken about me when I was just a baby, I had no idea of the amazing plan God was about to unfold for me and my family. Looking into Dad's weary, steel-blue eyes, somehow I could see all his prayers for me throughout my entire life, especially those born out of the pain of the past fifteen years.

But I could also see something else, something much bigger, much stronger—the face of a father who never wavered in the belief that his God can still bring thirty-three-year-old prodigal sons back home.

CHAPTER 1

BIG DREAMS IN A SMALL TOWN

Help me believe it
When I can't see it
Help me to know it
When I can't hold it[3]

In the summer of 2022, my parents, Steve and Jenia Williams, celebrated their fiftieth wedding anniversary. Quite an amazing accomplishment in any era of history, but especially in these past five ever-changing decades since they shared their vows before God in 1972.

Throughout our lives, they have provided me and my sister, Amy, with a firm foundation in Christ. In all my wayward years, while I was building my house on the sand, they had shown me how to live life on the Rock and, as Psalm 40 states, to "set my feet on solid ground." As Proverbs 22:6 encourages all parents to do, mine certainly trained up a child in the way he should go. So my story can't be told without talking about their stable and prayerful presence in my life. Without them, I would have had no idea that there was Someone to run to when I finally came to the end of my road.

My parents grew up in Bono, Arkansas (pronounced Boh-no, not Bah-no like the U2 singer). They became a couple when Dad was in ninth grade and Mom in eighth. Since they've been together, they've never been with anyone else. Even when Dad gave in to his own rebellion a few years later, he stayed faithful to Mom.

My mother's family owned a Phillips 66 gas station back in the "full service" days, meaning you pulled up and an attendant came out to pump your gas, wipe your windshield, even check your oil and tires. If anything was low, they took care of it. You never even had to get out of your car. (If you're under thirty-five, no, I am not kidding. This was a real thing back in the day.)

Their station was the preferred hangout for local farmers to stop in, grab a cup of coffee, and catch up on gossip when they came to town for supplies. But they all knew to stay clear of the mechanic's area, where a sign read, "Labor $15 an hour. $45 an hour if you watch." For many of the men in our community, the station was their gathering place.

Built on the interstate, the Phillips 66 was in a prime location about twenty miles from the nearest towns in either direction. It was a one-stop shop that sold car parts and offered basic maintenance like oil changes and flat fixes, as well as other minor repairs. On the side of the store were two attached bays to work on cars. The building was classic Americana, with Coke and cigarette machines out front. You could grab a Coke and a smoke while someone put gas in your car. I guess that's why they call them "the good ol' days," back before anyone knew that sugar and tobacco could kill you. And before they decided we were all perfectly capable of pumping our own gas.

Because Mom's family owned and ran the station, they had a very nice, large house, while Dad grew up in a small two-bedroom, one-bath home, sharing a room with his two brothers. He told me that he ate his very first steak when Mom invited him over to dinner with her family. Mom's family wasn't rich, but compared to the way he grew up, Dad thought they were. But even with that difference in raising, they were drawn to each other.

My parents got married when Dad was nineteen and Mom was eighteen. Once they were out on their own and away from their families, they experienced independence and some personal freedom for the first time. As happens with many young couples from solid, churchgoing families, they were lured into trying out the wild side.

Dad's family tree had two extremes, from alcoholics to preachers. But he had grown up in a strict home, so once he was out of high school, I guess some pent-up rebellion saw an opportunity to come out. Several of the guys Dad ran around with back then, even after he and Mom got married, eventually ended up in prison or died from drug abuse. Just in the past few years, he's told me some stories about those days when he started drinking, experimenting with drugs, and needing to come to grips with what he called an "addictive personality." He faced some tough crossroads of his own, and I think that's why he always found grace for me when, years later, he started seeing his old self in his only son.

Of course, substance abuse has been a temptation in every generation since humans first figured out how to create or consume anything that temporarily alters the mind. But the risk any of us take in using alcohol or drugs for the first time is that we have no idea how our bodies and brains will respond. For far too many people, it becomes easy to lose control. What starts out as fun, relaxation, or escape soon turns to abuse and addiction.

Because Mom had been raised in a well-respected blue-collar

family, when Dad went from social drinking out with friends to consuming heavily at home, that became a problem for her. She didn't mind him having a cocktail or two while hanging out with other couples, but getting drunk at home was not something she had signed up for. Those issues quickly took a toll on their marriage, and for about six weeks, they separated.

But, fortunately for me and my sister, it didn't take long for Dad to come to his senses. He realized he had to get away from the temptations to focus on putting his marriage back together. When my dad decides to start or stop something, he has always been able to do it. That unique resolve was a trait I later realized I had inherited from him.

Dad knew some major changes had to be made, and while seeking answers together, both he and Mom gave their lives to Christ. Even though they had each grown up in church, Dad decided he needed to give his heart to Jesus because Dad clearly saw that sin was destroying him. Realizing there is more to faith than just church attendance, they both chose to start a relationship with God. Their mutual decision would forever change the dynamic of our family for the better. To offer proof that Mom and Dad's transformation was real and lasting, I have never known my parents as anything other than strong Christ followers.

BUILDING A LIFE

Mom and Dad's new commitment soon led them to see the need for a fresh start, to begin a new chapter in life together.

So in 1977 they pulled up their Arkansas roots and drove away from the past to transplant in Pensacola, Florida. Dad got a job on a construction crew run by an older man there, doing framing and general carpentry. He had become skilled enough at his craft that finding work was never a problem for him. After they became established in their new city, Dad also started going to Bible college. He felt like some kind of ministry could be in his future and wanted to be better prepared for whatever God might call him to do.

As a part of their new beginnings, Mom and Dad decided they were ready to start a family. On June 27, 1978, I was born Zachary Stephen Williams. When I was just over a year old, Mom became pregnant with my sister. Knowing they were about to be parents to two small kids, with their marriage now strong and feeling like enough time had passed, they decided the best move would be to return to the support system of their families and community back in Arkansas.

So we left Pensacola and moved back to Bono, just outside Jonesboro. We lived with my grandmother, my mom's mother, while my parents built a house of their own. Our new home was at the end of a dead-end street, right behind my grandparents' house, just across from the city fire department where my uncle was the chief. I remember going over to the station all the time and marveling at the fire truck. Especially to a young boy, a fire engine, with all the red and gold, ladders and hoses, massive tires and doors, bells and sirens, looks like some sort of larger-than-life ship on which only heroes in huge, heavy coats and helmets get to climb aboard. Many nights I would be sound asleep in bed only to be suddenly awakened by the deafening siren. Looking up, I could see the flashing lights cut through the blinds on the window as the firefighters raced away to deal with danger.

As if that weren't quite enough noise, on the other side of my grandparents' house were train tracks. The 3:00 a.m. train sounded like it was racing and rumbling right through my bedroom. As many kids did back in the day, my buddies and I would take any pennies or quarters we could find and lay them carefully on the tracks. We couldn't wait for the next train to come through so we could go back and find our perfectly squashed and smoothed-out pieces of silver or copper.

The final detail of my Mayberry-like neighborhood was that we lived right beside the town's water tower, which had huge block letters of BONO sprayed in black for the world to see. Giving someone directions to our house was easy. We just said, "Below the water tower, across the street from the fire station, near the train tracks. Can't miss it."

My buddies and I played baseball all the time on the huge concrete driveway of the fire station. We always hit toward our house, but too many times someone would throw a wild pitch or a ball would tip backward off the bat and we would bust a pane of glass in the large rolling doors of the station.

My friends and I looked for ways to make our own fun anywhere we could find it. After a good rain we would wade into the large drainage ditch that ran right between the street and our front yard to catch crawdads that had been carried down with the runoff.

For a while, Dad worked for Mom's family at the Phillips 66. As a little kid, I spent quite a bit of time there. I remember the distinct smell inside that station—a mixture of oily rags, gasoline, and hot asphalt. I can still hear the loud ding of the bell when someone drove in for gas. Eventually, a builder in town helped Dad start his own drywall business. After being in construction for a while, he had decided to put all his energy into that specific area of construction. From there, he worked hard to get his company off the ground and quickly gained a solid reputation in the community.

Years down the road, Mom's family sold the gas station, but one of my cousins stayed on to run the business until 2023. It's amazing that this Arkansas landmark managed to stay connected to our family for decades.

In 1980, twenty-two months after I was born, my sister entered the world, making me the only Floridian in our family. Now raising two children, my parents began going to a new church plant that was meeting in a home. The pastor and his wife soon became Mom and Dad's best friends. My earliest memories are of our family in church together, going to the services at different members' homes. Everyone there became our friends, as we were together every Sunday morning and Wednesday night and often in between. The church became a major part of our family life. Before long, Dad started playing guitar and leading, with Mom singing in the worship band.

Because we had no church building in the early days, everyone gathered at the lake for baptisms. Those were always followed up by a big potluck picnic and cookout. I recall running around with my church friends, navigating through all the people, with the smell of grilling hot dogs and the sound of sizzling burgers giving us a huge appetite. Because we were right beside the lake, once we finally filled our plates, we'd have to fight off the flies and bugs from our food as we ate.

Music was an important feature of every church event. Because we were "charismatic," we didn't sing a lot of traditional hymns. Occasionally, we would sing the ones that had to do with God's power, like "Washed in the Blood" and "Power in the Blood." Most of our worship songs came from the most recent Maranatha! Music songbooks. Some of my favorites were "As the Deer" and "I've Got the Joy, Joy, Joy, Joy." If you aren't familiar with those, "As the Deer" is a ballad-style song taken from Psalm 42, while "Joy" is an upbeat, fun camp song.

The congregation soon became too big to meet in anyone's home. The church was eventually able to work out an arrangement to meet in the ballroom of a vacant motel. Now, with plenty of room to grow, stacks of chairs ready to set out for visitors, space for nursery and kids, and even women's *and* men's restrooms, the church was establishing roots in the community.

FORMING THE FOUNDATION

It's fascinating how small, seemingly insignificant moments forever lock into our minds as vivid memories. One of mine is the first time I saw an electric guitar. I can close my eyes today and still see it. I was with my parents at worship practice when a guy pulled a red Gibson Les Paul out of its case. Dad always had an acoustic guitar sitting on a stand at our house, but I never really paid much attention to it. It was just another fixture to me, like a coffee table or lamp. But *this* guitar immediately caught my eye.

I was mesmerized by the bold, rich finish, the trim outlining the edges, the curves on the body, the pearl pickups under the strings, and then the amazing sound that came out when he started playing. Up until that moment, all I had ever heard was acoustic guitars, so when he plugged the cord into the strange black box with all the knobs and switches, I was stunned to hear the powerful, bright, rich textures coming from something that still had only six strings. Even at my young age, the experience of seeing and hearing that guitar for the first time made a lasting impression.

At the worship practices for church, everyone's kids were there. As with many young congregations, childcare for any event was a luxury not yet possible. But there was something really cool about the community created when all of us were together. Listening to Mom and Dad and their friends make music to honor the Lord became familiar and comforting to me. As I played on the floor with the other children, I was literally surrounded by live music. A major part of my childhood was built around church and music, music and church. The two were intertwined and inseparable for me.

Another fond memory I have was my introduction to country music by my grandpa. I remember riding around in his van listening to his favorite eight-track tapes of legends like

Jerry Reed, Johnny Cash, and Willie Nelson. I always thought it was cool how he had his tape player mounted on the middle of the headliner above the dashboard where he could reach up and pop in a tape. In the back, behind the two front captains' chairs, he had built a bed frame with a mattress. Often my sister and I would lie back and listen to music while my grandparents were just cruising around. Those times were pure fun, creating such great memories.

My grandparents being music lovers, they often took me to gospel and bluegrass festivals in Mountain View, Arkansas. The town would have "Music on the Square," where people played all kinds of acoustic instruments. Those events were the first time I had ever seen and heard the banjo. The dulcimer. The mouth harp. The single-string tub bass. Whether people called it "mountain music" or "hillbilly music," whether the songs were bluegrass or gospel, to me, it was magical. Many of my childhood memories are of experiencing organic, live music played by musicians who obviously loved what they were getting to experience together.

When we went to the music festivals held at those small-town Arkansas downtown squares, there was usually a candy store where my grandparents would buy me some kind of sweetness-on-a-stick, and a bunch of ladies would be making quilts and crafts. Even though the town was in the middle of nowhere, no one cared because all those sights and sounds and smells were like being at the county fair. I think I loved the vibe so much because everybody was just so stinkin' happy! To me and my grandparents, those weekend days were awesome!

Listening to music was a part of my family's everyday life, from the records played at home to the car stereo always being on to the portable radio playing on Dad's job sites. In our living room, my parents had built their own entertainment center. They set two-by-eight boards across cinder blocks they had painted black to create a custom shelf configuration. The center held our TV, a vinyl player with speakers, and Dad's record collection. One trendy staple of the 1970s we had on one of those shelves was the lava lamp—a tubular glass piece with colored blobs inside, all sitting on top of a gold brass base. When you plugged it in, the light would come on, and the blobs would begin to move around and change colors. More than once, I accidentally touched the base and burned my hand.

The best part about our entertainment center was that my parents could change up or add whatever they wanted, just by moving the blocks and boards around. Another blessing of Dad being in construction was that our furniture could come from the local lumberyard, not an expensive showroom. Anything he made was not only custom but fit the budget too.

SOUTHERN SOUNDTRACK

Growing up, I spent countless hours sitting with my dad, listening to vinyls together. His collection consisted of just one genre of music—the still-new contemporary Christian music, or CCM. There were no phones, no screens, and no distractions back then, so we were totally focused on the singers' and musicians' talent coming from the needle in the grooves.

Because I have always loved to draw and sketch, I remember listening to Petra's albums and trying to re-create the cool graphic art emblazoned on their covers.

Another constant in our living room was Dad's guitar and music stand, where he always had Maranatha! Music songbooks with the guitar chords. He would go to the Lighthouse Bookstore in Jonesboro and buy the latest release of praise songs with the chord charts. I remember Dad practicing every week for Sunday morning, playing and singing through the songs, following along with the book open in front of him, perfecting anything new that would come out of Calvary Chapel's "Jesus music."

My first interaction with creating music was in the sixth grade in a gifted and talented class. The teacher told us about a national contest in which the school could win money if an original song by students was chosen for an antipollution campaign. Always up for a competition, I was all in. Because of my growing obsession with basketball, the title I came up with was "Shoot, Shoot, Don't Pollute." The lyrics were about picking up trash and shooting it into a trash can. Not knowing a thing about songwriting yet, I wrote it as a rap, which made it easier for everyone in the class to perform. We also came up with some simple choreography to go with the lyrics. When we felt like everyone had the song and dance down well enough, the teacher shot a video of us performing the rap. She then sent in our tape to the contest. Our class ended up receiving one of the awards, and we also got a check for the school. (That was the one and only rap song in my career . . . *so far.*)

When I was in seventh grade, Mom evidently decided that my sister and I needed a little culture. She made us both take piano lessons. I hated it. I did not want *anything* to do with it. But, with Mom ignoring my complaints, we took lessons for a whole year. The entire time, all I wanted to do was go outside to ride my bike, play ball, and hang out with my neighborhood buddies. I remember thinking, "Why in the world am I stuck in here taking piano?" Of course, now I'm grateful for what I did learn during that time and wish I would have stuck with the lessons. Today, I'm just dangerous enough on the keys to sit down and pick out an idea for a song.

By the time I was a teenager, one of the families from our church had a satellite dish installed at their house. That was a big deal at the time in small-town Arkansas. They would invite us over to watch the Hillsong Church service broadcast from Australia. I was blown away watching and listening to their worship team. That was back in the day when Darlene Zschech's classic song "Shout to the Lord" took the more progressive American churches by storm. We would also watch contemporary Christian concerts when they were shown on one of the faith channels.

Dad always listened to and searched for the latest worship music to teach to our church, so he was continually introducing me to the latest artists in contemporary Christian and gospel music. He played me some who are now legends and heroes of mine, but Dad often discovered them back when their first albums came out.

The biggest game changer for me was when we got a VHS

tape of Mylon LeFevre and Broken Heart's "Sheep in Wolves' Clothing" live concert. Watching incredibly talented rockers sing unashamedly about Jesus *rocked* my world. Mylon has always had such a killer, classic, Southern rock sound. I also had the cassette and was constantly listening to him and his band. "Trains up in the Sky" is still one of my favorite songs of all time.

Another artist that heavily influenced me at a young age was Russ Taff. My dad first listened to Russ when he was with the Imperials. During Russ's incredible solo career, I wore out his *Walls of Glass* record. Some of my other favorites were Petra, as I mentioned before, and also DeGarmo and Key. I was eight years old the first time Dad took me to see Eddie and Dana perform in Memphis. The idea of merging rock music with the gospel was sinking down deep into my heart. And I don't think anyone had more influence on what would eventually become my vocal style than Mylon and Russ. Obviously, I had no idea that, from a kid into my teen years, all those artists were shaping what would become my own sound, years down the road. Just more proof that God can end up using anything and everything.

Yet, even with all these artists' positive influence and strong impressions on me, I had no desire to play music. Playing music was my parents' thing. In grade school, basketball became my passion. Especially in a small Southern town, my generation was particularly biased toward guys becoming jocks and not "band nerds," as they were called back then. Ironically, far more young people from my generation went on to make a living playing music than those who became pro athletes.

While our family certainly wasn't rich by any means, my sister and I never wanted for anything. My parents were amazing providers. We were the classic example of 1980s and '90s middle-class America. Dad's construction job, along with Mom's work as a beautician, then her eventual switch to being a dental hygienist, always offered a secure living. Later, my mom decided to start college and get her nursing degree. During our childhood, rather than bearing the expense of sending me and my sister to day care or hiring a sitter, Dad would often just take us to his job sites. Going with him to work was just as normal to us as being at home. Amy and I would play together while he worked.

If you already know some of my story, you might be surprised when I say that my childhood was about as close to perfect as any family could offer. I don't have bad memories of any hurtful events in our home.

END OF THE INNOCENCE

Starting around the fourth grade, with each passing year, as I grew bigger, I became better at basketball. That created expectations of me being not just good but great. While those expectations were likely formed mostly in my own mind and heart, I felt like the bar was set really high, that I needed to stand out. The more I excelled, the more pressure I put on myself. I started feeling like I had to live up to a standard

I didn't know if I would be able to reach. My identity was starting to be formed by a performance mindset—based not on who I was but on what I could do.

My life's dream of playing basketball in college and then going on to the NBA became stronger as I got older. That goal became everything I wanted out of life. My father and my uncles had been standout athletes in school. Dad had made the all-star team in high school and played in junior college. Because I wanted to follow in their footsteps, I would eat, sleep, and breathe basketball. If I had any free time, no matter the weather, I was out shooting hoops.

While basketball was the dominant and positive force in my life, I began to rebel and get into trouble. In such a small town, the biggest problem for me and my friends was sheer boredom. The age-old argument of, "Everybody else is doing it," dominated our thinking and decisions. If I wanted to hang with my buddies, I had to do whatever they did.

This dynamic with my friends started an ongoing conflict with my parents around junior high. I realized my friends were getting to do some things I wasn't allowed to do. I noticed that my buddies had more freedom than I had. Like most kids, I didn't have the maturity to realize that my parents loved me and were trying to protect me. I couldn't see that some of the guys' parents should have cared more instead of just saying, "Sure, go do your thing. Whatever."

I struggled with resentment toward Dad and Mom for not letting me hang out as long as I wanted or do some of the things I wanted. For example, if I asked to go somewhere with a buddy, I might be told, "Well, we don't know his mom and dad, so we're not letting you go." I would often come back with, "But so-and-so gets to go!" And they would answer with, "Well, so-and-so isn't our kid."

I always had a curfew, which was usually earlier than everyone else's. Being the first one to have to stop the fun, to leave and go home, was hard. The more that happened, the more rebellious my heart became. While I was never out of control or a bad kid, sometimes it felt that way because I couldn't do what others could or stay out as late as they did. Was I somehow going to get into more trouble than them, so I had to be contained more? But along with the rebellion came a sense of guilt and shame for anything I did that I knew my parents wouldn't approve of—all the feelings that the enemy loves to use against us. It's the classic "frog in the kettle" story. The heat turns up so slowly that eventually you don't really notice what's happening in your heart.

When you grow up in a small town, often there's not really a reason *why* you do anything you do. But because you say yes to just wanting to have some fun, you can also unintentionally introduce problems into your life that you won't know how to stop down the road. Because we lived at least an hour away from the nearest major city, peer pressure, or whatever you want to call it, caused me and my friends to get into trouble, like stealing cigarettes or, later, a six pack of beer. We always saw the older kids doing those things and figured that's just what you do in this town. Everyone wanted to fit in, so we all just settled for status quo and followed the pattern that had been set for years, all with what I thought was just innocent fun.

While my parents were strict on one hand, in other ways they would show me way too much grace—mostly by believing what I told them. The bigger problem was that I became a convincing and creative liar. One particular night, I was supposed to be home by a certain time. I had no excuse for being late because my parents had given me a watch. Running way past my curfew, I put my watch down into some water until the face got soaked enough to fog it up. I walked into the house with the excuse of being late because I couldn't see what time it was. Anything to stay out of trouble. Funny how as lies get easier, life gets harder, because lying ends up taking way more work than the truth.

Back then, smoking was still considered "cool," so my buddies and I would come up with a plan to steal a pack of cigarettes from the neighborhood convenience store. We would meet up and walk down the train tracks that led straight to Kelly's IGA grocery store (IGA—Independent Grocers Alliance). Walking in, one of us would buy some candy and ask that it be put in a small brown paper bag. While the clerk was busy with the candy transaction, one of us would sneak a pack of cigarettes. The rest of us just wandered around the store to create a distraction. Then we would conceal the cigarettes in the paper bag. We could then smuggle the cigarettes unnoticed as we all walked out together. This was obviously before products like cigarettes were kept behind the counter. (Kids like us are probably why those laws exist.) Next, we had to figure out a safe place to hide the pack and also plan a group smoking session. All while thinking we were such clever thieves.

One time Dad found one of the cigarette packs hidden in our doghouse. When he asked me what I knew about it, I told him the cigarettes belonged to one of my buddies and that he smoked them, not me. I swore they weren't mine and that my friend had hidden them in there. Dad appeared to buy my story. Fast-forward to a few weeks later, when my buddies and I were hiding behind our shed in the backyard, smoking. One of the guys started picking up plums that had fallen off a nearby tree and throwing them against the shed. Dad was inside the house taking a nap. The sharp pop of those plums hitting the wall woke him up. When he came out to see what was going on, there we were. Of course, the moment Dad came around the corner, he zeroed in on me. He glared at the other guys and, with a stern voice, said, "Y'all need to put those out and leave . . . now." My buddies were more than happy to do what he asked, throwing their cigarettes down and running home.

After they had left, Dad looked at me and asked, "What's that in your hand?" Ashamed, I looked down and put out the cigarette on the ground. But he insisted, "No, go ahead and have another one." I responded, "No, Dad, that was enough." But he had decided he was going to teach me a lesson. "Yeah, Zach, you *are* going to have another one." Dad stood there watching as I nervously lit up a cigarette. As soon as I put one out, he would tell me to light up another. Finally, when I reached the point of getting sick, he said, "Okay, that's enough.

Since tomorrow is your twelfth birthday, I'm not going to tell your mom that I caught you doing this, because it would break her heart."

Man, did I ever get sick! What Dad didn't know was that when I "smoked" with my friends, I never actually inhaled. I faked it. But with his punishment, I now understood the feeling of having your lungs full of smoke and the horrible burn as if your throat is on fire.

Let me rewind a bit and go back to the doghouse story. The reason Dad had found the cigarettes in there was because he was cleaning it out after my dog had died. This wasn't long after Halloween, and some of my sister's guy friends had toilet-papered our house, then grabbed my dog and spray-painted him blue. *Yeah, blue.* He was never quite the same after that and passed soon after. One of those boys eventually became my brother-in-law, and so I have often used that prank to my advantage by telling him, "You know, when I was a kid, you killed my dog."

BATTLE ON THE BROAD ROAD

My parents probably knew a lot more of what I was doing than they let on, but I also understood how much they loved me and wanted to believe I was always telling the truth. They didn't want to face the fact that their son was making bad choices and lying to them. But, like many kids, I learned I could get away with certain stuff with Mom and other stuff with Dad. I had figured out how to play that game.

By late elementary into middle school, while the battle for my heart was constant, the God of my parents was always present. I began to not want to go to church because most of my friends didn't. Anytime I would ask to stay home, or sleep over at someone's house on a Saturday night, or ask why my parents were making me go, the answer was always, "As long as you're living in this house, you're going to get up and go to church on Sunday." That would usually trigger me to say, "Well, I can't wait to get out of this house, to move out, so I can do what I want to do!"

But on the other side of that coin, I can remember in certain church services how I would sense or feel something strange spiritually. I'm not sure if it was the Holy Spirit or just my emotions, but I would find myself fighting back tears, wondering, "Is this the way I'm supposed to feel? Does everybody here feel this?" I'd slip away to the restroom and then hang out in the hallway until the service ended. Those feelings were confusing and a little scary. What I felt in church was clearly conflicting with what my buddies and I were doing, and then the lying just made everything worse. In those vulnerable moments, I would fight the urge to go down front at the invitation. Whenever I did give in to the urge, I waited until other people went down first. I have always been an introvert and never liked drawing attention to myself (an interesting paradox about many artists who perform live that most people don't realize).

With my choices slowly eroding my innocence and my desire for independence growing, the stage was now set for my flesh to start putting up a good fight to beat out my spirit. I had to deal with the constant reminder that I knew better than to act how I was acting. A consistent voice inside told me, "This is not how you were raised. This is not what God has for you." But some bad seeds were being planted. Roots of rebellion against authority were sprouting. I had no idea at the time just how tough and bitter the coming harvest would be.

CHAPTER 2

FREE THROWS AND PERSONAL FOULS

All the times that I worked hard because I believed
That life could have meaning through things I've achieved
You knew . . . I was looking for You

Every time I thought romance might fill up the hole
That incomplete feeling still ached in my soul
Oh, You knew . . . I was looking for You[4]

B y the sixth grade, I knew there was something more to my athletic ability. I started to realize I was the best player on our basketball team. By seventh grade, I was taller than all the other guys. And then between ninth and tenth grade, I grew six inches. I went from an even six feet tall to six feet six. As you can imagine, a fifteen-year-old that tall gets a lot of attention on a basketball court. At that height, while weighing in at 175 pounds, my body was certainly cooperating with my dream of playing pro ball one day.

But, for some strange reason, there's a dynamic that happens too often in youth sports: I had a high school coach that didn't understand kids at all. He had none of his own, and his approach was constant anger, taking it out on the entire team. If you're a basketball fan, you'll know his coaching role model—Bobby Knight. A lot of screaming, yelling, kicking stuff, throwing things, throwing fits . . . *that* guy. For my coach, there was little difference between a good day and a bad day. To be fair, he did have one strength—his knowledge of the game.

I was never sure why, but he didn't want anyone on his team to stand out; he thought every player should be the same caliber. His lack of people skills, with no desire to encourage and nurture boys, could take a player with promise and turn him into mediocre at best. Because of his coaching style, he and I didn't get along. My dad or I would often try to reason with the coach after a game. Yet nothing ever changed. Little did we know, the coach was keeping some kind of score regarding our issues with him.

FINDING MY VOICE

In high school, my increasing rebellion against authority began to affect my taste in music. I wanted to listen to songs that expressed how I felt inside. So, parting ways with the Christian music I had listened to with my dad, I got into metal bands like Marilyn Manson, White Zombie, Pantera, Korn, Ozzy Osbourne, and Rage against the Machine. Chris Cornell from Soundgarden became a big influence on me. I liked the aggression, the attitude, and the angst in both the sound and the lyrics. The ironic thing is I had nothing to be mad about, but I think being in the middle of the MTV generation fostered a general sense of agitation and a middle-finger attitude toward society. (Back when MTV was actually music videos, not reality shows.)

As strict as my parents were, they never policed the music I listened to. I remember my dad bought a *Hit Parader* magazine that had a feature article about Marilyn Manson. Dad was just trying to figure out what Manson was actually about. After he read the piece, he told me, "This is basically just David Bowie or Alice Cooper back in the day. It's just another 'shock rock' artist doing crazy things for media attention." Obviously, he was watching what I was doing and listening to, but my parents never tried to stop me. Well, except for one time, Mom found a rap record when I was in eighth grade and told me I couldn't listen to it because it was too raunchy. I just wanted music I could sing to and use to blow off steam, turning it up as loud as it could go and raging along to the songs. Regardless of the musical genre I was into at the time, the common thread is that I have always been drawn to powerful and passionate singers.

Just like I would join in whatever my friends did, I would listen to whatever music was popular. We all listened to the same artists. The darkness in a lot of the music intrigued me. Even though I understood that most of the bands were just a gimmick, I was attracted to the theatrics used in a lot of the concerts at that time. When I went to a White Zombie show, I was blown away by the level of their production. I was beginning to pay attention to all the other aspects of a great show besides just the artist's performance.

I think watching music videos and listening to the songs stirred something inside all of us Gen Xers. It made us feel like we belonged to something. Like we were part of something bigger. Something we *chose* to be a part of, not something we were *told* to be a part of. My generation seemed to have an attitude of, "Man, let's go! Turn up the music! Let's turn up life as loud as we can!"

During my sophomore year, I started singing along to my favorite songs. And when I say singing, I mean not holding back at all. I would belt out the lyrics, just like the guys I was listening to. The more I sang, the more I realized I had a decent voice. That changed my perspective on music. I left the metal bands behind and got into straight-ahead rock, particularly Southern rock. My uncle had introduced me to Lynyrd Skynyrd, Gov't Mule, and the Allman Brothers Band. I loved singing along with those soulful, smoky, raspy guys like Ronnie Van Zant, Warren Haynes, and Gregg Allman.

A friend of mine on the basketball team would often pick me up for school in his car. In my driveway we would start "Welcome to the Jungle" by Guns N' Roses, and it would end right as we pulled into a parking space at school. My buddy said, "Zach! That's crazy! You sound just like Axl Rose! How do you do that with your voice?" I had no idea because, at first, I was just singing along. But times like that made me more comfortable singing around my closest buddies. I listened to the Guns N' Roses *Appetite for Destruction* album all the time, so taking in what my friend said, I worked on mimicking Axl's vocals on every song on that record.

Other than those few guys, I never wanted to sing in front of anyone. At church, I would sing only when I knew I could blend in with the crowd. I already had the town spotlight on me when I was on the basketball court, so music was just my little secret escape from the day's troubles. After I got my driver's license, cranking up a cassette and singing along as I drove created a great distraction from stress. I would get lost in the music, belting out every song.

As I sang more and more, particularly with the records from Southern rock bands, I realized I could make my voice sound like most of the guys I listened to. I started to work at copying their styles and nuances. In some proud moments, I thought, "I'm matching this guy note for note." I discovered later that it's common for young singers to mimic or impersonate their favorite artists, partly because they may have no idea yet what their own voice actually sounds like or what their style is. I also started experimenting with "runs," where a singer ad libs, turning one note into as many as they want. Some of the artists who became famous for incredibly acrobatic vocal runs in that day were Celine Dion and Whitney Houston. A more current example is Chris Stapleton, whose voice I love and am constantly inspired by.

So, under the radar, I was learning to sing long before I ever thought about picking up a guitar. From the time I started driving until going away to college, I was unknowingly, unintentionally developing my voice. To me, I was just having fun, while virtually no one else, including my parents, even knew I was singing.

Even still, I never gave music a second thought. Basketball was my life, with no plan B.

MEDICATE MY MIND

My relationship with substance abuse made its introduction into my life when I was in the sixth grade. That was my first taste of alcohol. On the night of our sixth-grade graduation, someone had a huge party. My friends and I found the parents' liquor cabinet and took turns trying out Scotch, peach schnapps, and whatever else we felt like no one would miss.

The last bottle we tried was Cutty Sark whiskey. That night, we all realized the effects of booze, and we liked it.

As my friends and I ventured out more, the opportunities to get into trouble increased. During those years, for us, drinking was always just a crime of opportunity when someone made it available, or at least accessible, and the situation appeared to be "safe," meaning we could keep it hidden from parents and coaches. At that point, we were all just experimenting. The first time I got drunk wasn't until the ninth grade.

By my sophomore year, a few parents would buy alcohol for us as long as we agreed not to leave the house that night during a sleepover. One Friday night, we had a bottle of both Jack Daniel's and Malibu Rum, plus some Red Dog beer. I distinctly remember the rum tasting like the smell of suntan lotion. For several years, I had a picture that was taken of me that night. I was sitting on the arm of a couch with a lit cigarette in one hand and the bottle of Jack Daniel's in the other and a chew of Levi Garrett in my jaw. I was shirtless and wearing a cowboy hat.

In that picture, the look on my face made it seem like I was having the time of my life. When all my friends were drinking, life felt fine. Life was fun. No holds barred. I thought it was awesome because I didn't have to be in control of anything. We could do whatever we wanted and say whatever we wanted. Of course, this was back when teenagers weren't recording every single moment on their phones and sharing with the world.

I had finally found a way to escape from life—the

ever-growing standards, the hard-to-reach expectations, and the constantly increasing rules. At these parties, I didn't have to think about basketball or grades or *any* responsibility. The crazy part was we would get drunk on Friday nights and then wake up early to be at our basketball games on Saturday mornings. That was my introduction and indoctrination in how to get smashed and then, just a few hours later, have to be on top of my game, literally.

While my parents probably assumed we were misbehaving in some way, they had *no* idea what was really going on. They thought it was just innocent fun—watching movies, eating junk food, staying up late, and, of course, playing basketball. We did do those things, but alcohol was always the featured activity.

Because we lived in such a small town, I started driving at fourteen years old. I got my first car when I was fifteen—a 1991 silver four-door Cutlass Supreme. *Yes, I had a car before I got my driver's license at sixteen.* I saved up money from anytime I worked for Dad and put on some American Racing chrome rims. The ashtray was always full of loose change, so every time I hit a big bump, the tray would fall open from the latch not being able to hold the weight. The main reason my parents let me have a car before I got my license was so I could drive to and from school, basketball practice, and local games. Because they both had to work full-time, the car allowed me to get where I needed to go on my own. Back in the day, kids in small towns driving at that age wasn't unusual.

Also in the tenth grade, I was introduced to marijuana by

some of my basketball teammates who were a year older than me. One Saturday, five of us were in my car, driving down a gravel road on our way to another buddy's house to play video games. We had the Arkansas Razorbacks football game up loud on the radio.

One of the guys had crafted a pipe out of a Mountain Dew can. Because we were in the middle of nowhere, I slowed down to around fifteen miles an hour. We knew the nearest cop would be miles away. My buddy set some weed into the can, lit it up, and we took turns smoking out of the hole on the end. When my turn came, I had one hand on the wheel and the other holding the can as I smoked for the first time. Sounds strange, but I thought it tasted like sausage. *Random, I know, but that's what I recall.* I was surprised that, unlike alcohol, it didn't take long for me to feel the effects.

When the sports announcer on the radio counted down the final seconds of the football game, the Razorbacks had won. My buddy riding shotgun reached over, grabbed the shift lever, and threw my car into park, causing my Cutlass to lurch to a halt. He threw his door open and started running around the car, screaming, "Hogs win! Hogs win!" Between the weed and his craziness, we were all laughing uncontrollably, now parked in the middle of the road. I thought, "Man, this is freakin' awesome! This is the best feeling in the world!" I knew in that moment I had discovered yet another way to escape and medicate.

All of us in the car were on the basketball team. But we weren't doing anything that everybody else in our school wasn't doing. At least, that's what we all thought. Because of that attitude, none of us believed that getting drunk or smoking weed was bad. In my mind, it was hard to find someone who *wasn't* drinking and smoking. It just wasn't a big deal to us.

An important truth I had no way of understanding yet was that I would be chasing after that "first time feeling" of getting high for the next twenty years. I've talked with many folks about this strange dynamic. From the second time to the last time, regardless of how many years are wasted in between, always chasing that amazing initial feeling becomes the goal you can never seem to reach. This is why many people unintentionally overdose, thinking, "Maybe if I do just a little more this time."

HIGHS AND LOWS

Getting high relieved the stress of reality and allowed a reprieve from all the teenage drama and pressures, especially the constant tension that was always there with my coach. Also, while my dad didn't realize what he was creating in me, his expectation of my basketball performance became a constant weight. I know he never intended to make me feel like I had to live up to a certain standard, but I certainly took it upon myself to try.

Being a parent of teenagers today, I fully understand and appreciate the difficult balance of motivating and encouraging your kids versus applying pressure and demands. That's a tough line for any parent to walk. But all those emotions and toxic feelings just fueled my growing desire to escape.

The pressure I felt from my dad was only the beginning. Because we lived in a basketball town, with my size and ability, I always felt like I had to be the best. From my coach on the sideline to all the people in the stands, I was very aware of what everyone wanted from me in every game—to win. My performance was not important just to me but also to all of them. So the weekend nights filled with drinking and smoking with my buddies allowed me to have a space where I didn't have a care in the world. But once the brain experiences that kind of relief, it wants more, which then turns into too much. There's an old saying that goes, "Two's too many and one's never enough." So true.

As with many people, for me, smoking pot started out as just an every-once-in-a-while thing but soon turned into more. In one of the compartments in my car, I hid a pipe, a little glass bowl. I would keep it packed with pot. As soon as basketball practice was over and I was in my car alone, I would get it out, light up, and take a hit. Depending on how high I got, I would hang out with a friend or stop by a buddy's house until I came down enough to go home. High schoolers can't usually get away with being "a little drunk," but that was another advantage with pot—I could still be a little high and Mom and Dad wouldn't notice.

What starts out as "recreational" and fun slowly becomes an apathetic attitude of "Well, this is just what I do." Reminds me of the old joke, "Marijuana isn't addictive. I ought to know,

I've been smoking it every day for the past ten years." While the substance itself may not be, the desire to be high certainly is. I am also convinced it is a gateway drug.

I told you earlier about Dad's discovery when I had lied to him about cigarettes. One particular weekend the mess I got myself into was on an entirely different level. My friend Eddie and his mom were about to move to Cabot, Arkansas, two hours away. His little Isuzu truck was in my family's service station getting a new water pump. I had asked my parents if I could ride with Eddie to Cabot for his first weekend there. Because we would have to drive on the interstate, they told me the only way that could happen was if we followed his mom when she went.

But Eddie's mom ended up leaving the day before his car was ready. Talking it over, Eddie and I decided there was no way we weren't going to Cabot that weekend. What kind of trouble might we miss out on? And we had to go see if the girls in Cabot were prettier than the girls in Jonesboro. That next morning, as soon as Eddie's truck was fixed, we took off, supposedly following his mom.

About an hour outside of town, almost halfway there, Eddie's truck broke down. We were stranded on the side of the interstate. This was well before every teenager had a cell phone. We had no way to let anyone know we needed help. So we sat on the side of the road and discreetly smoked one of the joints we had brought. Finally, we decided to start walking to find help. About four or five miles down the interstate, we came to a little town and walked up to a house not far off the road. We knocked, and a nice couple came to the door. After we explained what had happened, they let us in to use their landline phone to call home. Needless to say, when I had to explain what happened and answer the question, "Where is Eddie's mother?" Dad and Mom were *not* happy with me.

While Eddie and I were waiting for my parents to arrive, the nice couple made us lunch and broke out their daughter's yearbooks to show us pictures of her. Evidently, she was about our age, so while they had a captive audience, they gave us the full history of her life. When Mom finally arrived, she explained that Dad was back at the truck, trying to figure out what was wrong. We thanked the nice couple for their hospitality and made the death march to the car.

Meanwhile, Dad had found a pack of Marlboro Reds in the truck. That would have been bad enough, but then when he opened it up, he saw that one of the "cigarettes" was actually a joint. Once Eddie, Mom, and I came back outside, we all got in the car for the long drive home. No one said a word. Total silence. I knew I was in trouble with a capital T. But I didn't know about Dad's discovery yet.

When we pulled into our driveway, Mom and Eddie quickly got out of the car. Dad didn't budge, so I decided it would be best for me to stay put too, still sitting in the back like a statue. He looked at me in the rearview mirror and pitched the Marlboro pack over the seat to me. I caught it and opened it to see the joint still there. That's when he asked, "So, you're smoking pot now?" *Okay, buckle up, here we go.* I swallowed hard and answered, "No, Dad. Eddie collects Marlboro miles off the packages to exchange for prizes. When we were on the side of the highway, he found the box in the grass. I didn't even look in it." *Yeah, just like that. Another huge lie.*

Dad appeared to buy the story. He didn't say another word, so I assumed my explanation was enough to satisfy him. After all, who could make up such a crazy story on the fly like that? But those were the lengths to which I would go when I was cornered. Right on cue, I'd come up with a wild yet somehow believable story. Don't get me wrong. I'm not proud of it, just being honest.

In those days, I constantly rationalized my marijuana habit, thinking, "There's no real harm in this, and it's not like I'll do it forever. Someday down the road, my life will change and I'll give this up." When you're young, "down the road" seems so far away. Meanwhile, all I knew was that I was having the time of my life and somehow getting away with it all.

CRASH AND BURN

Going into my senior year of high school, our basketball team was the favorite to win the state championship. Scholarship offers from universities started hitting our family's mailbox. My picture, play-by-plays, and stats were now routinely in the local newspaper. Life was lining up perfectly for my high-school-to-college-to-NBA dream to come true.

But then everything changed on what my friends and I thought would be just another typical fun night hanging out together. The "no harm, no foul" attitude was about to end.

Early in the season, a bunch of us on the team were at one of the guys' houses studying for a big test. The cheerleaders were going to come over to study with us after their practice. Ready for a break, we decided to pile into a car and go wait on them to finish practice and then we would all go back to the house. We sat waiting for them in the car in the dark and mostly empty school parking lot. One of the guys had brought a joint, and before long, he lit it up and started passing it around to all of us. We were *all* smoking. By this time, it was nine o'clock at night with no one in sight. When the girls finally came out after their practice, they got in their cars, and we all headed back to the house to study.

The next day after school, we decided to go to a basketball game across town to watch another school's team play. After we got to the gym and found a spot in the bleachers, we soon started hearing buzz from other kids that somebody had ratted us out about the night before. Someone had told our coach what we did on school property, and he was going to make us all take a drug test first thing the next morning. Being just six games into my senior season, I was freaking out. My teammates and I were trying to figure out what was going on. It didn't make sense that any of the guys in the car would have said anything. So who told? Not to mention, why? *Why* would anyone do this to the team?

Every morning at 6:15, our team met in the gym and went through a shoot-around drill for about an hour before classes began. That next morning, the coach was acting strange. He was pacing back and forth, ignoring us. Never said a word.

When our hour was up, we went into the locker room, got ready, and went to class.

By third period, I was in home economics when, over the intercom, each one of us guys was called by name to the office. I was terrified because I had no idea what was about to happen. Adrenaline took over my body, as I assumed this was about the rumored drug tests. We had to sit outside the principal's door, waiting to be called in one by one. The sheriff was there, along with the superintendent, principal, and, of course, our coach and his assistant coach. One at a time, they were interrogating us. Keep in mind that none of us were eighteen yet and no one's parents had been called.

As I was sitting outside the office, waiting my turn, my best friend, who eventually became my brother-in-law (the alleged blue-dog sprayer), came out the door, crying. He looked at me wide-eyed and said, "Dude! They know *everything*!" Shocked, I asked, "What! How?" He said, "Yeah! There's a list with our names. Some have checks by them and some are circled."

When my turn came to go in, one of the men looked at me and said, "Williams, we already know what you've done. We just need you to admit it." But the story and the accusation had gotten out of hand from rumors and bad information. They were claiming that we were buying and selling drugs in the locker room, which none of us had ever done.

After the grilling was over, they finally called my parents, and my mom came to the school. Out of everyone that confessed, only three of us—me and my two best friends—were punished. We were the seniors, but also the "stars." They told us we were not only kicked off the team but expelled from school too.

Whether it was small town politics, or the coach wanting to make an example out of his best players, or both, we couldn't understand why this was happening in this way. Why were only three of us taking the fall for a carload of guilty teammates? The next day my name was in the newspaper for a very different reason than it usually was. In our tight-knit community, this became a huge ordeal, like, scandal-level stuff.

At the time, I was dating a girl, a typical high school romance where you think you're in love. Right after the story spread, I went to a basketball tournament to watch some teams play. I was standing alone when my girlfriend's dad walked up to me and said, "You can't see my daughter anymore." Shocked, I responded, "But sir, she's been my girlfriend for a long time. I'm at your house every weekend. You know me. I'm like one of your own kids!" He just glared at me and said, "Stay away from her. Do not call her again. You aren't welcome in our home anymore. We don't want you around." Just like that, this upstanding Christian family wrote me off. I thought they might show some grace or even forgiveness, but the small-town peer pressure was just too much. Stronger than faith, apparently. I was suddenly the Arkansas version of a leper.

The toughest part for our family was the friends who suddenly assumed the entire story was true and distanced themselves from us. Too many people wanted to avoid "guilt by association." Not many folks came to my parents to find out the other side of the story, proof that cancel culture was alive and well long before social media came on the scene. Because everyone knew everybody's business in a small town, it was strange to see the hypocrisy of a lot of the adults who pointed fingers at us. I knew some did much worse things on a regular basis.

In those dark days for our family, Dad reflected on a lot of the moments when he had found something of mine or questioned the truth in the stories I had told him. With this crisis at school, he was putting two and two together. One night he came to me and asked, "So, back when I found that pack of cigarettes with the joint in it? You were smoking pot back then, weren't you? You lied to me, didn't you?"

I knew all my defenses were gone. The truth had to finally come out, and I confessed it all. In that moment, I realized how "nauseated" my heart had been for a long time, and that's why it finally felt good to "throw up" all the lies I had worked so hard to hide. As a parent myself now, I cringe when I think about all the times I lied to my mom and dad. Many nights I would come home at 12:30 a.m., blowing past my curfew again. Mom would be waiting up and ask, "Zach, why do you smell like cigarettes?" Without missing a beat, I would answer, "We were at Ron's Pool Hall. Lots of people were smoking there." Or she would ask, "Why are your eyes so red?" Even though I was stoned, I'd say, "I was around a lot of cigarette smoke tonight and it irritated my eyes." But then I would go straight into the kitchen and spend the next half hour eating everything in sight. Even though I was a growing teenage boy, the "munchies" were a telltale sign.

An attorney heard the story about me and my teammates and called my dad to offer his counsel. When we met with him, he told us that handling underage boys the way the school did, not allowing any parents to be present during the interrogation, and then letting the story leak to be published in the local paper warranted a lawsuit. But we didn't want money. We just wanted to get me back in school and back on the team so as not to jeopardize my future basketball scholarship. So as not to jeopardize my future, period!

Our attorney went with us to speak on our behalf at a *very* public school board meeting that was called only to address this issue. While backing down on the severity of the original decision, the board still held to a ten-day suspension—two full weeks of school. But no basketball. That was over.

As news of what happened spread, because my name was well known in high school basketball around the state, I quickly started getting offers from other schools. They said things like, "Hey, if you'll move into our district, we'll put you on our team *now*! Over here, we understand that kids are going to make mistakes and should get a second chance."

Seeing those offers as an opportunity, Dad and I started looking for a short-term lease apartment in some of those other school districts. It was amazing that my parents were willing to forgive me and make the sacrifice of temporarily moving to keep me in school and keep my basketball dreams alive. But that plan didn't work out because anywhere we could find to live was either too expensive or not in a safe area.

Weighing out everything that had happened, I made a life-changing decision, a massive choice at only seventeen years old. I made the call that I wasn't going to serve the ten days and then go back into that school, especially not being allowed to play ball. Their lack of fairness and the retaliation from the coach and administration was more than I could stand. I wasn't going to let them have the satisfaction of seeing me in the hallways. Plus, I couldn't take a chance on some other accusation being raised down the road that might prevent me from graduating.

I made the decision to drop out of school my senior year before Christmas break. My parents were fully supportive of my decision. They understood the need to distance myself from the school. In three days, over the holidays, I took all the necessary tests and got my GED. I lost all hope of a basketball scholarship. The calls stopped and the offers were rescinded. My ultimate dream of one day playing pro ball appeared to have died that day in the principal's office.

Now, had I done something in that school parking lot that I should not have been doing? Had we *all* done something we shouldn't have been doing? Smoking marijuana, an illegal substance according to our state law, on school property? Yes, absolutely, guilty as charged. But fairness was thrown out the window, with only three of us going down for the team.

Oh, and the drug test? I passed. And my negative result was publicly presented at the school board meeting.

While we never found out the full story, we suspected that a kid on our basketball team that rarely got to play had been the one to start the fire by telling the coach. But then small-town politics took over and poured on the gas to stoke it into a full-on blaze. Of course, that type of thing doesn't just happen in Arkansas, it's everywhere. Paul nailed it in Romans 3:23: "For all have sinned and fall short of the glory of God" (NIV).

PAIN AND POISON

Uncertain of what to do next and still in shock about how quickly life had turned on me, I went to work full-time for Dad, putting up sheetrock. Knowing most of my friends were at school enjoying their lives and celebrating their senior year, I thought, "Man, my life is over. Everything I've worked so hard to become, everything I wanted to do with my life is gone. Just like that. Literally, up in smoke."

If only someone in that circle of authority could have offered us a shot at redemption. But now that was history. I harbored resentment toward that coach and all those folks for a long time. That's a lot to handle at seventeen years old. The analogy of living in a small town being like living in a fishbowl is accurate. With so many friends turning their backs on us, even Mom and Dad, as mature Christians, struggled with bitterness as much as I did. Many years later, my mom told me that it took her a couple of years to forgive everyone involved.

Fortunately, as a star volleyball player, my sister, Amy, survived the family scandal. Her team won several state championships. I did my best to encourage her to avoid making the same mistakes I did. She was able to go to college on a volleyball scholarship and play on a Junior Olympic team. I'm so glad she got to have those experiences.

But, as for me, feeling like I was an embarrassment to my family and the community, with my dreams shattered and my motivation to succeed gone, I saw no reason to clean up my life. In fact, by the time I turned eighteen that summer, I felt like I needed the numbing effects from any substance, legal or illegal, now more than ever.

The betrayal and abandonment I felt drove my rebellion to a far deeper level. I went from living it up in high school to living a lifestyle that led to destruction as an adult. This was my fall from grace. This would start my downward spiral. But in a very real way, this was also where my rescue story would begin.

CHAPTER 3

Got to Run to Keep From Hiding

Hard times and high waters on the road that I have wandered
Bridges left burning, a lot of dead-end learning
Stone walls I've built up, trapped by the way I'm living
I don't wanna be a prisoner[5]

You might think that something as traumatic as the blowup at my high school would have gotten my attention to set me on the straight and narrow. But the difficult crossroads any of us face in life, especially those involving pain that we struggle to overcome, tend to drive us in one of two directions. One is to move away from the behavior and find a path out and upward. The other is to sink deeper, to just give in and give up. Unfortunately for us as broken people, the second option is usually the easiest—the path of least resistance.

In this fallen world, running often wins out over resting, and hiding over healing.

After putting up drywall all day with Dad, I was out partying at night and on weekends. Thinking I was just harmlessly hanging out with friends, my parents had no idea I hadn't learned my lesson from everything our family had gone through. They would have been surprised and heartbroken to know I was worse off than ever. Without schoolwork or any sort of accountability, I had way too much free time and money in my pocket to stay out of trouble.

But basketball was still in my blood. Fortunately, what happened at school didn't cause me to give up on the game itself. Because it felt like my only safe and familiar place, I loved playing now more than ever. A ball in my hands and a net in front of me seemed to be the one calming constant I could count on. I knew *exactly* what to do with a ball. Life, not so much. That's why when I found out about a local men's intramural league, I signed up right away.

In January, when all my friends and ex-teammates were beginning the final semester of their senior year, I was walking into a gym to meet my assigned team. As soon as I entered the gym, all the familiar sights and sounds made me smile. The fresh lacquer on the floor reflecting the bright lights. The sound of shoes squeaking as the players made their quick starts and stops. And the unmistakable swoosh of the nothing-but-net three-pointers. Except this time I wouldn't be competing with peers but with grown men up to fifteen years older than me. Watching for a few minutes, I could tell there were some serious players on this court, requiring me to bring my A game.

One day, after all the games were finished, a man walked up to me and asked, "You're that Williams kid, right? The one who got into trouble and kicked off the team?" Really tired of that story being attached to me and not sure where he was going, I just nodded. He continued, "Well, if you think you can keep your nose clean for awhile, I believe I can get you a tryout at a junior college in northwest Arkansas. You interested?" *What?* Now this stranger had my full attention. "Really? College?" He smiled and answered, "Yeah, I played ball there. . . . Just promise me you won't mess this up, okay?" Surprised and shocked, I agreed. "For sure, I promise."

Both smiling, we shook on it. I couldn't believe how a local intramural game had brought a new opportunity to get me back on the road to my dream, which was something I *never* thought would happen, especially so quickly. I continued to play in that league through the winter into spring until, just like he promised, the guy came through. He called and told me I was invited to a summer tryout to be considered for a couple of open spots for North Arkansas College in Harrison.

On the day of the tryouts, Dad and I drove the four hours to the school campus. When we walked in and met everyone, I realized I had played against several of these guys in high school. They all knew who I was and what had gone down at my school. They started joking with me, asking, "So, you think you can still play ball?" I was so ready to put the past behind me and have a fresh start that as soon as we got into a game, I left it all on the court. Knowing my future was on the line, with Dad and the coach watching, I brought my best, hitting at least seven three-pointers. I played what may have been my best game ever that day. *I gotta tell ya, that felt really good.*

When the tryout was done, the coach walked over and told Dad and me that he would seriously consider me for one of the available spots for the fall and that he would be in touch. A few weeks later, he called and offered me a full-ride scholarship. A full ride!

So, by being in the right place at the right time in the intramural league, I was now back on track with my original plan of making basketball my career. I would start college in the fall, the exact same semester as my graduating class, as if nothing had ever happened. God had answered my parents' prayers and was clearly giving me a second chance at my dream.

Even though my scholarship was connected to sports, I knew the degree I wanted to pursue. With a pro basketball career now back on the table, my goal was to get an art degree. Because the junior college didn't offer graphic design, I opted for the next closest subject—commercial art. My mom has always been really creative, painting pictures and doing all sorts of craft projects. I inherited that talent and skill from her. Starting at an early age, as I mentioned before, I loved to draw and sketch. I remember being in church as a kid, sitting around my buddies, doodling on the bulletin during the sermon. They would often look over and say, "Whoa, Zach, that's really good." Like singing, it was just something I enjoyed that created a fun distraction. But to keep playing basketball, I needed a major, so art was my natural choice. I was aware I had artistic talent and also knew it would be a lot more fun than other studies.

Party 'til Practice

I left home for the first time, moving four hours away. I hadn't given much thought to what college life would be like, but I was not at all prepared for the level of temptation I would face. I had basically gone from the frying pan into the fire, as they say. It didn't take long for me to see that what got me kicked out of school and off the team, what me and my family had been ostracized because of, *everybody* here was doing every single day. Drinking. Smoking weed. Drugs. Partying. The students here acted like this was just normal life—certainly not anything you could get in trouble over!

Now I had not only a lot more temptations than in high school but also total freedom to do what I wanted, when I wanted, where I wanted, and with whom I wanted. No in-your-face coaches. No nosy community. No rules. No reputation to uphold *or* escape. And no one knew me. Here, marijuana was a given, just a starting place. Not a big deal like back home, for sure. People were into all kinds of substances I had never seen, much less smoked, inhaled, snorted, or swallowed. I was still in Arkansas but living in a *very* different world.

My student housing was set up by the school. Across from the library were apartment-style units for students, with two bedrooms each. There was other athletic housing, but I was assigned on campus for my freshman year. My roommate was also on the basketball team. Three guys who lived nearby kept everyone supplied with weed.

I was living for free, *and* my parents were sending me spending money. So before long, with little responsibility and all the wrong kinds of opportunity, I was partying every night. *So much for the second chance.*

That first month in college, I don't think I ever went to class sober, and certainly never not hungover. I would be up all night partying and then try to make it to school in the morning. Fortunately, all my classes were just a short walk from my apartment. A few weeks into the semester, before basketball season had even started, my coach pulled me aside after practice. Apparently, someone had told him that our trash cans outside were always overflowing with beer bottles. Calm but serious, Coach said, "Zach, you've already got egg on your face from high school. Don't mess up this shot at college. You need to get your act together, okay?"

My surprise was not really that he knew what was going on, but more his approach. This guy was night-and-day different from my high school coach. High school basketball had involved yelling and screaming, with practices mapped out to the minute. Full-on high stress. My college experience was more like, "Here's the ball. You guys get out there and play." Even still, after the coach's easygoing warning and obvious grace, I didn't slow down at all. Just like lying to my parents, once again I just got better at hiding.

With so much access and excess all around me, I started to push the boundaries even further, going from one party to the next, one drug to the next. *Nothing* was off-limits. I tried just about anything that promised some kind of high or out-of-body experience. The first time I tried acid was right at the end of my first semester when some friends decided we should drive to Silver Dollar City, near Branson, Missouri, and look at Christmas lights while tripping. As you can tell by now, I was careless. I just did not understand what I was doing to my body and the toll it was taking on me. I *never* considered the consequences, ever. Always living *in* the moment, *for* the moment, I was becoming self-destructive without being suicidal.

In my first year of college, I watched many guys who had never drank, smoked weed, or partied get mixed up in this lifestyle. I don't believe any of us thought about the future. I certainly never considered this to be something I would keep up when I got out of school. But that's the trap of sin, right? You choose to start something, but then it seems you can't choose to stop. When we're young and away from authority, a false sense of being bulletproof can easily override any sort of common sense. Curiosity coupled with a lack of fear is a dangerous combination. Living that way can easily come back to bite you. It's a miracle I survived those days.

One of the craziest parts of this season of my life was that because my buddies and I were athletes, we were able to get away with just about anything. Everybody knew what we were doing, but everyone looked the other way—the exact opposite of what I had experienced in high school. To us, it felt like being small-town celebrities. A lot of the issues we've seen in the news in recent years about college sports was beginning to happen back then, even in small colleges. When a school makes money from sports, the athletes are taken care of, one way or another.

I had become *that guy*. The one always trying to impress everybody with how far he can go. The class clown. The wild man. The loose cannon. I didn't think the party could start until I got there. And I didn't think it could end until I went home. That gave me a reputation for always being in the middle of everything. Thank God, in all the craziness, I never became dependent on any substance. My only addiction was attention. I chalked it all up to, "That's just my personality." I was very competitive on the basketball court, and that attitude transferred to any activity where I could try to outdo someone. If I was going to do *anything*, I was going to do it better than *anybody*. So, for example, if someone set a whiskey bottle on the table, I was going to drink more than anyone else. My drive to win on the court came with me to every party.

Yet even in all the craziness of my lifestyle, sometimes I would be in a situation I knew I shouldn't be in, and suddenly, without warning, I would feel God's presence. Whether that was conviction or guilt, I wasn't certain, but I'd often wake up with regrets and shame for what I'd done the night before. Those feelings were often strong, and I would wonder if they meant God was calling me back to Him or trying to protect me.

Still, somehow, I would push those thoughts and feelings back down and not allow anything to take hold; I just kept going in the wrong direction. *Why?* The only answer I can offer at this point was that I hadn't hit bottom yet. I was still having too much fun to change.

Six-String Distraction

The day before basketball season was to start, the coach had us do a walk-through practice—running drills and plays but not going full speed. Seeing that we weren't going to run, I didn't take the time to lace up and tie my shoes. When one of my teammates went for a layup, I jumped in front of him to swat it away. I blocked the shot but came down on the guy's foot. With no ankle support and the awkward landing, I tore all the ligaments in my ankle. Yeah, no joke, *all* of them.

Within seconds, my ankle swelled up and looked like a softball had been glued to my foot. Just like that, I was out for my entire first season of college basketball. I didn't play a single game. I couldn't believe it. Another bad break from a stupid choice. But this time, it wasn't because of something I had done but something I *didn't* do. If I would have just stopped and taken the time to lace up and tie my shoes correctly, I might have had enough support to keep from injuring myself.

But that hindsight didn't matter now. Basketball was out, and a lot of inactive downtime was my new normal. I was forced to redshirt my first season and didn't travel to the majority of the road games. With all the unexpected time to recuperate, I knew I would have to find something to distract myself from going stir-crazy.

One day, while home alone, I looked over and saw my roommate's old Harmony acoustic guitar leaning against the wall. I thought about all the years I had seen Dad's guitar sitting in the corner. But then I did something I had never done with his guitar. I decided to go over and pick it up. I sat back down, seeing how it felt in my hands. To the best of my recollection, surprisingly, I had never held a guitar before. Immediately, something just seemed right, oddly familiar, like two strangers who meet for the first time but can quickly tell they're going to become good friends.

After messing around on it for a while, picking single notes up and down the neck, I tried to remember some of the simple chords I had seen Dad play. Ready to take on this new challenge, I decided to go to the music store in town to find a good beginner guitar manual. After looking through several, I bought a classic Mel Bay chord book. Starting with his first release in 1947, Mel's books became the bestselling instructional guides for guitar, using pictures, notations, and finger diagrams. His book laid the foundation for every chord I would ever play.

The first song I learned to play all the way through in tempo was Bob Dylan's "Knockin' on Heaven's Door." But because of the style of music I was into at the time, I learned Eric Clapton's rendition. My second song was a fingerpicking version of "Blackbird" by the Beatles. I know I must have driven my roommates nuts playing those same songs over and over again, trying to play them perfectly. I soon discovered that countless classic songs use only three or four basic chords. That's part of the beauty of music: the simplicity *and* diversity.

Next I bought a large poster of a comprehensive chord chart and pinned it up on my wall at the end of my bed. Before long, I was getting serious about the guitar and, ultimately, making music, something that likely would never have happened if I hadn't gotten hurt. All the hours I had been dedicating to basketball were now going into learning the guitar. The strange thing was, up until that point, I had never been interested in music aside from listening and singing along. (And the *last* thing I was thinking about was learning a future job skill.) Yet, there was no mistaking that, from the moment I held that guitar in my hands, I was drawn to the instrument. Maybe it was because of my first impression as a kid seeing that Les Paul at my parents' worship practice. Or the familiarity of Dad's guitar growing up. Regardless, a powerful connection had been made. While I couldn't explain the feeling, I just knew there was something right about this new interest to which I committed more and more time and energy.

After I had been playing my roommate's guitar for a while, I went to Memphis to the famous Beale Street Music Festival. Watching and listening to all those incredible blues players inspired me even more. On the way back to school, I stopped in to visit my parents. During the catch-up conversation, I asked Dad, "Hey, I'd like to take your old Epiphone guitar back to college with me. Is that okay?" He was visibly surprised at my request. "Okay . . . but why?" I smiled and answered, "Well, I've been teaching myself to play guitar." He laughed and said, "Well, son, my Epiphone won't be very easy to learn on."

At that point Dad had been playing for decades. The guitar I asked him for was his twelve-string. He knew those are much tougher to play because instead of each finger holding down one string at a time, it has to hold down two. But, because of that, the sound is epic when all the strings ring out in tune in a solid chord. What I didn't tell Dad was that my plan was to remove six of the strings and just keep the main ones. Because I'm a big guy, wrapping my fingers around the wider neck on the twelve string was exactly what I wanted.

Back at college, I made the modification to Dad's Epiphone. I was so ready to give my roommate back his Harmony and grateful to have my own guitar. Now I could take mine with me anywhere I went, anytime.

By my second year at school when the next basketball season

rolled around, I was healed up and playing at one hundred percent again. But everything had changed. I only stayed on the team to maintain my scholarship, because I felt like I owed it to my family, with school being paid for. My focus and attention had done a one-eighty shift. At twenty-one years old, for the first time in my life, I couldn't care less about basketball. All my passion had transitioned to music. I was so consumed with it that I remember one college professor telling me, "If you spent half as much time on your art as you do playing music, you'd be a really good student." I heard that comment several times after I had decided not to become a graphic designer, but I didn't care because all I wanted to be now was a musician.

TRIPLE THREAT

Once I became comfortable with the muscle memory of changing chords, I started to add my voice to the mix. All that work on singing in secret since high school was now going to pay off. While I was learning to play and sing songs, I realized I didn't want to just perform other artists' material. It was like I knew there was something in me that had to come out. That's when I started to write my own songs. Once I began that creative process, music took root in my soul.

My next semester, I decided to take a creative writing and poetry class to become stronger at penning song lyrics. I would take poems and stories I had to write for class and join them up with my growing list of guitar chords to craft original songs. Now that I was merging my playing and singing with writing, I became better at all three. These were the first steps to me becoming not just a singer or a guitar player but an artist.

The very first song I wrote was called "Tribal Times," taken from a poem I wrote for my class. At the time, like all rookie songwriters, I thought I had just written the best song in the world. Here's a verse and the chorus. Pay attention to the theme here. Feel free to read between the lines.

———————————

Stand beside me
Look into my eyes
When you're with me
Can you see my disguise?

I'm traveling through these tribal times
And I'm walkin' on a road I've been before
Oh, I'm slippin' through the hands of time
Like a grain of sand along the shore

———————————

When I discovered the outlet of songwriting, I felt like for the first time in my life I had an authentic way to express myself, a way to get my feelings out, to let my emotions escape by creating my own message through a melody I had written. I soon realized I had a lot I wanted to say, feelings I normally wouldn't tell anyone or talk about. In a song, I could disguise my feelings in the lyrics, but people also seemed to relate to what I was sharing. Performing a song I had written started to feel even better than winning a basketball game. Once the desire to create had a pathway out of my heart, it has been a constant in my life. That's why, even today, my preference is songwriting over performing live, likely because, by nature, I'm an introvert.

The first time I ever played in front of an audience was my junior year in college. My graphic design class had a couple of guys who were also musicians. At our fine arts center one night, we had a gathering of about thirty people where I played a song I had written. One of the other students accompanied me on guitar.

One day in the creative writing class, I showed up and realized an assignment was due. Because I had forgotten and didn't have time to write an original poem, I took the risk and quickly wrote down the words to a Creed song and turned that in for my assignment. Fortunately, the professor didn't recognize the lyrics and gave me a good grade. I guess the positive to that story is he didn't see a major difference between a rock hit and what I had been turning in. I thought that was a good sign.

From metal in high school to Southern rock in college, my tastes began to also include the blues. Besides going to Beale Street, I also went to the Eureka Springs Blues Festival. I couldn't get enough of live music. I was blown away by the players. I think everything I had been through up to that point drew me to the blues—a way to express pain with no apologies, a take-no-prisoners type of music. Like I said, I've never been one to easily talk about how I feel, so expressing what was in my heart, whether passion or pain, through a song was like medicine to my soul.

Next I went to a Black Crowes show, and then the ultimate—I got to experience the Allman Brothers Band live. Man, was I ever hooked. My taste in music was broadening and opening up a whole new world for me. My attitude at parties shifted to become a little less about getting the most drunk or high and more about playing in front of people. Not that I stopped doing any substances; I just added music to the experience anytime I could. Whenever I went out, I always put my guitar in the back seat. Often someone would say, "Hey, Zach, get your guitar. Play one of your songs for us."

FOOD FOR THE SOUL

Before I had left home to go to college, my mom had given me a cookbook and said, "Zach, you're going to need to learn how to cook for yourself. I won't be there to do it." At school, I lived around a bunch of guys who were all hunters from the mountains of Arkansas. They were always bringing in wild game from a weekend hunt and grilling out. They taught me how to cook various meats. With that, I learned the art of seasoning and preparation. Soon, making a meal became another form of creative expression for me. I began to see the value of sitting down at a table and sharing food with friends.

Hearing them say, "Man, this is awesome" or "This is the best spaghetti I've ever had" was so rewarding.

Whether it was a tableful of friends enjoying a meal or a group of people hearing me sing an original song, the positive response and immediate feedback were fun to hear. Both music and meals have a great return and reward. When you make something, you usually create it for yourself. But what you create you can also share. Whether you're drawing a picture, writing a song, or cooking a meal, like in sports, if you put in the work, you'll win your game. That's why playing cover songs was never satisfying to me. It was just performing something someone else had created. Kind of like microwaving a meal; it just isn't the same experience as fashioning it from scratch.

By playing in front of people, I also quickly realized I could get the attention of everyone in the room, most importantly, all the girls. To me, I was already partying like the rock stars I listened to. I had the lifestyle down. After all, the "sex and drugs" comes before the "rock and roll." I just thought that's what you had to do to be a musician—live to excess.

While the music did attract a lot of girls, they would come and go quickly. After a while, they each saw that I cared about music far more than I did about them. By the end of my sophomore year, I had also decided I didn't need sports anymore. Basketball would always be fun to play, but now that ship had sailed. I was a musician. I only identified as an artist—what I saw as the new and improved plan for my life. The decade from the age of ten to twenty years old had been committed to sports. Now my twenties were fully committed to playing music. The guitar became like another part of my body, and my new purpose in life was playing, singing, and writing songs.

I started writing songs in 1999. By 2005 I had thirty complete songs. One weekend me and my buddy, who had a small recorder, put them all on tape. I would say the title of the song, then in one take each, I played my guitar and sang every song. I took that tape and sent it to Washington, DC, to secure an official copyright. Eventually, I received a letter with a government seal telling me my songs had been registered with the copyright office and could be legally protected. To this day, I have every one of those songs in a folder on my phone. In fact, I have *every* original song I've ever written in that folder. While, of course, my music has changed from that first song to today, you can still hear my same style and how I've stayed true to who I am.

Somehow I managed to last two years at North Arkansas, both surviving the partying and making good enough grades to pass. I got my associate's degree in commercial art and knew I wanted to move on to a bachelor's degree at a school that had a strong graphic design program. The closest university was Arkansas State in Jonesboro, not far from my parents, where I enrolled for my last two years.

Moving back in with my parents, back to the town where everyone knew me, I would have to get better than ever at hiding my lifestyle. The substances I was accustomed to doing were far worse now than when I had left after high school. So

I had to figure out how to walk the tightrope of being good around the good folks while still being bad with the party crowd. Like a chameleon, I would have to change colors quickly to blend into my environment. But one thing was for sure—no matter where I was, I had *zero* desire to change.

CHAPTER 4

BETRAYAL, BLUNTS, AND THE BLUES

When he told you you were troubled, you'll forever be alone

When he told you you should run away, you'll never find a home

When he told you you were dirty and you should be ashamed

When he told you you could be the one that grace could never change

Fear, he is a liar[6]

My parents are baby boomers, so they are of the generation that taught their kids there's never a good and acceptable reason to throw a pity party. You just don't do that under any circumstances. Stop the whining, stop your crying, pick yourself up, and move forward because no one else is going to do it for you. I had this classic, old-school American mantra on repeat in my head: "Pull yourself up by your bootstraps." Looking back, I believe at times I was genuinely depressed, but I never acknowledged it. I didn't want to allow myself to have those feelings, even though I was clearly struggling. The thought "What do you possibly have to be depressed about?" would ring in my ears. A lot of us Gen Xers deal with those dynamics, especially those of us raised in the South, with that mindset being a part of the culture.

During the second semester of my junior year at Arkansas State, for the first time in my life, I was serious about a girl. I thought we were exclusive and that the feelings between us were mutual. But my world was rocked when I found out she was cheating on me with one of the fraternity guys. *A frat boy? Seriously?* I didn't see it coming, so the breakup was brutal. Her betrayal totally messed me up because it was my first real heartbreak.

With the incident at my high school, the injury in junior college that diverted me away from my basketball dreams, and now this toxic end to what I thought was a real relationship, it was becoming easy to feel like a failure. Devastated, I slipped into a depression and began drinking and drugging even more. I added Xanax to my arsenal to try to numb the emotional pain. That was also my first experience with illegally using prescription drugs. I didn't want to leave my parents' house. I didn't want to see anyone. Through all the grieving, I had no appetite and lost twenty pounds. Yet when anyone would ask me how I was doing, trying hard to keep up the bootstraps mentality, I would always answer, "Fine. I'm fine." But inside I was a train wreck.

While the competitive side of me still knew I had every opportunity to be anything I wanted to be, I was daily drowning in a flood of negative thoughts and emotions. My constant sense of high expectations fighting with the failures kept hamstringing me. I felt like a screwup and didn't know what to do with all the emotional baggage. I looked for more ways to make me forget, even if only for a few hours. But that's when the very things you're running from can begin to take over and shape who you are.

I couldn't see it at the time, but whenever I would try to get back up and take positive steps forward, something would knock me back down, taking my feet right out from under me. Of course, some of those were self-induced, but others I had zero control over.

While in this wounded state of mind, with only thirty credit hours remaining in my bachelor's program, I made yet another drastic decision. I quit the university. I dropped out just two semesters away from crossing the finish line. Leaving high school and surviving probably made bailing from college that much easier. Once again, something traumatic happened to me, and I took the first off-ramp. From school to relationships to partying, I was badly burned in life. That is, except for one thing—my music. That was the only semblance of hope I had left. The only path forward I could see to escape my life. The only way forward that might lead to any sort of success.

The final straw that made quitting feel like my only option was news from my degree counselor. She informed me that because I had no existing art portfolio to present for graduation, I would have to retake a class. That was my fault because whenever I created any kind of art project, I would give it away to someone. As a result, I ended up with nothing to show. When she told me I would have to take that class over again, I was so ready to play music that I didn't even consider continuing my education, especially if it meant adding another semester. Much like I abandoned basketball for music, I now made the same decision with my art. My mind was made up.

FROM PANIC TO PASSING OUT

Checking out of school, I went back to work for Dad full-time again. He made room for me in his business, part-time or full-time. The positive for Dad was he could always use the help and never had to train me. I could show up and step right back into the job, knowing exactly what to do.

By this time, drug dealers were experimenting with stronger, more potent product, as well as lacing drugs with narcotics and chemicals. A few times I got hold of a batch that was mixed with meth or some other substance I had never experienced before. The first time that happened to me, I couldn't stop shaking. Even my teeth were chattering. It's terrifying to realize some unknown drug is in your body and you have no idea what it is, what it will do to you, or how long it might take to work itself out of your system. And you won't know until it is too late, and then your only choice is to ride it out. And, of course, there's always the fear that this time might kill you.

One time I was getting ready to go to a friend's wedding. I had gotten high and started ironing a dress shirt. Within a few minutes, a full-blown panic attack hit me. My mind was racing. I had trouble breathing. My heart was pounding so hard and beating so fast that I thought it was about to explode. That experience freaked me out to the point that I finally decided I had to try to quit. I told myself, "That's it. I am done!"

Over the next year, anytime I tried to smoke pot again, a panic attack would come. After it passed, I would stay away for a while, out of fear. But those episodes were the only thing that stopped me. Fortunately, I never experienced that feeling of "I can't live a day without it" with alcohol the way I had with pot. While I drank ridiculous amounts for many years, I never woke up craving a drink. In fact, because of how horrible I felt from the night before, I would often tell myself that I should never touch the stuff again. But then, by that evening, I'd be over the hangover and ready to go another round.

On the night of my twenty-second birthday, a buddy and I drove to Mississippi for a Kenny Wayne Shepherd concert. After the show, we decided to go to a club we had seen as we drove into town. We thought it would be funny to lie and tell any girls we met that we were on Kenny Wayne's road crew. We hadn't been there long when a girl approached me. I was already on my way to drunk at this point, and it was obvious. She asked me if I wanted to go in a back room with her. Of course, I agreed.

As soon as we were alone, she started making out with me. I thought I had hit the jackpot. She suddenly stopped and asked me, "Have you ever done GHB?" I had no idea what it was, but I lied and answered, "Oh, yeah, all the time." She smiled and said, "Awesome. Hang on, I'll be right back." What I thought was the greatest thing ever on the night of my birthday was about to get ugly. What I didn't know was that GHB is often used as a date rape drug—really serious stuff—but I was clueless.

Soon the girl came back with a little foil pipe that obviously had weed packed in it. I watched as she placed a few drops of GHB on the pot, lit it, then handed it to me to smoke. I should have paid attention to the fact that she didn't partake first. I smiled and took a big hit.

Three days later—*yes, three days*—I woke up in my buddy's trailer back in my hometown. As I cracked my eyes open, I tried to figure out whether I was actually alive. Assuming heaven or hell wasn't in a mobile home, I figured I must have survived whatever happened to me. After I finally saw not just the time of day but also the date, I realized I had missed two days of work. This was one of those situations where my parents had probably begun to think the worst—that I might be dead—because they couldn't reach me or find me anywhere. I caused them that horrible fear too many times.

As I tried to piece together what had happened, suddenly I remembered the last thing I had done—a big hit on the pipe while the girl was watching me like a buzzard waiting on roadkill. Immediately, I felt for my wallet. It was gone— everything—driver's license, cash, and credit cards. As I sat up on the bed and put my feet on the floor, looking down, I noticed that the toes of my boots were badly scuffed and worn down. "Well, that's weird," I thought.

My friend told me the whole story and explained the condition of my boots. After I passed out, the girl robbed me. Then she went and got the bouncers, who were likely in on the scam. They grabbed my arms and dragged me out of the club and through the parking lot, then threw me down by my friend's car. The only thing that had touched the ground were the toes of my boots. That is, until my face hit the gravel. He said I had been in and out of consciousness for the past three days, but I had no memory from my puff on her pipe to waking up. Here was another incredibly stupid thing I had done and yet another time the Lord had protected me to live another day for still another shot at His rescue.

For some reason, the panic attacks finally stopped, so over the next seven long years, I don't think I went a single day without getting high. We've all heard the term "functioning alcoholic." Well, I became a "functioning pothead." I didn't want to try to navigate life sober. That's why I would go into crisis mode anytime I realized my stash was running low. Anxiety would overwhelm me, and an immediate bad mood would set in. Those feelings would last until I found someone with a joint or scraped together enough money for a new supply. I didn't want to even think about waking up in the morning without something to smoke.

During that season in my life, several times I watched my buddies shoot up heroin. But I could never handle needles. I drank and did drugs to escape reality while awake, not to pass out. I wanted the feeling of being high, not anesthesia. Watching them sit in some dumpy trailer in the middle of nowhere and stick a needle in their arms to go into a coma was never my idea of a good time.

Through much of my twenties, I was like Bill Murray in the movie *Groundhog Day*. Except I wasn't figuring out how to make *anything* better. Instead, life was getting worse. After I left college, I would wake up, smoke a bowl, go to work, break around ten o'clock to smoke a joint, work until lunch, eat, smoke another joint, work, take another smoke break midafternoon, work, go home at five, and then try to stay high until whatever time I went to bed. The next morning, I would get up and do it all over again.

And the whole time, I was trying to dodge Dad and sneak around at the work sites. I tried hard to hide the smoking from him. It helped that he didn't want to believe I was getting high on the job. I do recall one particular day when he grew suspicious about my appearance and decided to confront me. No surprise, I lied like always. Once again, I was convincing. I swore I wasn't high—I was just exhausted. As was our pattern, he trusted me and I took advantage of his grace.

All day, every day, my job was to mix up buckets of drywall mud, take a trowel, and apply the mud to every sheetrock seam in every room. I was constantly staring at white lines on gray walls and smelling the strong, distinct odor of a dried-in house under construction. Staying stoned was the only way I could endure the monotony of my life. Even though I was still writing songs and playing occasionally at parties, at this point, I just assumed construction work was all I would ever do for the rest of my days. I had no reason to think anything would ever change, and I certainly wasn't trying to make anything different happen.

I remember one specific day when I was working on what is called a "corner bead." That's the metal strip that connects the sheetrock in the corners of the room. When you put the mud down that strip, the whole goal is to get out all the bubbles and little pits until you have a perfectly smooth texture. When you mud the seams, you also want to do all you can to minimize having to sand it later. As I kept running the trowel down that corner, I thought, "Is this really all there is? Is this going to be my life for the rest of my days? I've always thought there would be something better for me someday, but will there?" Maybe that corner bead felt like a metaphor, making me feel particularly cornered in life.

The only way I knew to keep going was to stay high, and

now that wasn't even fun. It just became what I had to do to manage and medicate myself to keep going. The thought of doing this work sober was more than I could handle. My dad had always had a purpose in his job—to honor the Lord and take care of our family. I had no purpose and saw no future. I had no reason to show up, except to make a buck. I thought by my midtwenties I would be at a very different place in life.

Once I finally decided to give dating another try, I met a girl and started my first serious relationship since the one in college. We ended up being together for seven years, from the age of twenty-two to twenty-nine, when my life was just working and partying, doing drywall and smoking joints. Over time I had worked through my fears about love and developed real feelings for her. But then, here we go again. I found out she was cheating on me with the guy we bought our drugs from. *The drug dealer? Seriously?* I had been played again. Betrayed again.

Because I had put my bandaged-up heart on the line only to be betrayed a second time, my fragile ego was shattered to pieces. I was on emotional life support. Both times, I had become overconfident in the relationship, falsely thinking, "Why would somebody cheat on me? I'm the best thing she's ever going to find. Plus, I'm going to be a rock star someday." But no, my first serious relationship was ruined by a frat boy, and now my second, by a drug dealer. Life was going from bad to worse. My love for playing the blues made more sense than ever.

By this point, to say I had developed major trust issues

RESCUE STORY

would be an understatement. After the first cheating incident, I had shut down. Now this time, I not only closed my heart for business but also boarded it up with plenty of safeguards for security. Like a man trying to protect his house from an approaching hurricane, I told myself, *Nothing is getting through here ever again. I will never be with anybody, ever. I never want to hear another woman say, "I love you." If she does, I'm out.* That was my new creed. If a girl ever said, "I love you," that would be a warning shot that I was about to get hurt. Sure enough, a while later, I was set up with a girl and we went out a few times. One night she told me that she loved me. Immediately, I glared at her and said, "I don't want to hear that. I'm out!" I ended it right there and even stopped talking to her. Case closed.

A Guy Walks into a Bar

One night I went down to a club to drown my sorrows and hear a local band called Further Down. They had a publishing and licensing deal with song placements on some Nickelodeon shows, as well as a single being played on a local radio station. Their first album had been released, and as happens with many new bands, what they thought was going to skyrocket ended up being just a bottle rocket. Nevertheless, they had become a big deal in our area of Arkansas, and I wanted to hear them.

I was in the bathroom on one of their breaks when the bass player, Red Dorton, walked in. After I complimented him on their set, we struck up a conversation. I told him I was

80

a singer-songwriter and played guitar. When we went back out, he introduced me to the other guys. To my surprise, they invited me to play a song before they started their next set. Of course, I agreed, borrowed one of the guitars, and stepped behind the mic. Singing at all those parties for years had shaved off any shyness or insecurities I had. I decided on an Eric Clapton cover just to play it safe for a bar crowd. Because no one knew who I was, I wanted my first song in a club to be a win. *Can't go wrong with Clapton, right?*

At the end of the night, as I talked with the guys, Red said, "Hey, dude, you sound pretty good. We're having a party tomorrow night at the house. You should come by and bring your guitar. Let's play some music." Looking for any chance to perform anywhere for anyone, I said yes.

The next night, I walked in with my guitar case in hand to find about fifty people crammed into the living room. When they invited me to play, I took out my guitar and launched into one of my original songs. Halfway into the first verse, everyone had stopped talking and turned toward me. Nobody said a word. They were all listening. I could tell by looking at the guys in the band that they were intrigued that I had gotten everyone's attention.

After I had done a few songs and thanked everyone for listening, the guys gathered around me. "So, Zach, what's your story?" I went into my own version of what probably sounded like the lyrics to an old blues song. I was honest with them about my current circumstances and how I was back at square one in my life.

All of them except the lead singer lived together with some other guys—nine people in a five-thousand-square-foot house. When I had finished telling them my story, Red said, "Well, we just had a guy move out. You can take his room if you want." They told me what my rent would be each month, which I could swing. (Any rent divided by nine is pretty affordable.) Just like the game in the intramural league when the guy walked up offering me a shot at college basketball, here was another random intersection in my life. One night I walk into a bar, meet a band, get invited to a jam, and land a cheap place to live in a houseful of musicians. I grinned and accepted their offer: "Dude, that would be awesome!"

After moving into their house, I started trying to figure out a way I could also move into the band. I began tagging along on their gigs as a roadie. Just like had happened at the bar, they started asking me to come up and do a couple of songs between sets. Then they wanted to back *me* as I sang. Soon, at every show, they would tell the crowd, "Hey, we're going to bring up a buddy of ours to play with us. Everybody give it up for Zach Williams." I would walk on, and we would launch into the Allman Brothers Band classic, "Midnight Rider." Playing together night after night, we got that song really tight. When I came up, the lead singer would step to the side and sing harmony with the other guys.

Without the distraction of a relationship in my life and time on my hands after work each day, I got busy writing new songs. As soon as I came home, I would head downstairs to write and record on the little rig they had set up in the basement. Because of this arrangement, the guys were always the first to hear my songs. That is, everyone except their singer, the only guy in the band who didn't live there. They were excited about my writing, so we started putting the songs together and rehearsing. Before long, I could see that this new version of the band was going to work. The more songs we learned and got tight, the more they invited me up on stage for longer sets.

At that time, their look was sort of an alternative vibe. But I was wearing Western-style shirts with pearl snaps and bell-bottoms with cowboy boots. With long hair and a beard, I had this Southern-cowboy-hippie look going. After a while, they started buying those kinds of clothes too, changing their image. An up-and-coming band at that time was the Black Crowes. We started to pattern ourselves after them. As we got to know one another and the more songs of mine we learned, they got on board with the new plan. Eventually, they wanted to start playing the songs we had worked up instead of the ones they'd been playing. The guys in the band were ready for a new sound. In a matter of weeks, they came to me and said that their singer had decided to move on and wanted me to take his place.

By the time the guys invited me to join the band, we had worked up enough of my original songs to record an entire album. That alone changed the game for the band. They realized I could likely offer a ticket out of playing small clubs and hopefully get us where they thought their first album was going to take them but didn't.

Besides the original songs, I also brought a different philosophy to the live show. The guys tended to jam on songs and improvise a new version every night. They wanted to shred and stretch out in long solos. But with me taking over the front man spot, I told them, "Guys, people don't pay money to come and hear you noodle. We are *not* the Grateful Dead or Dave Matthews Band. They come to a show to hear the originals the way they are on the record. Take REO Speedwagon, for example—they're still playing those same songs the same way every night, the way they were originally recorded and played on the radio. I know it might be boring to *you*, but it's just what we have to do to get a solid reputation among fans."

They didn't like me toeing that line, but I knew that was a key factor in separating the good from the great, the cover bands from the recording artists. By that point, I had learned that as a performer I'm not up on stage to play for *me* but for the people who paid good money to see and hear me.

In 2007, when I was twenty-nine years old, I was finally on the road playing music as a front man, lead singer, and songwriter. We were all "weekend warriors," meaning we still had our regular jobs during the week. Fortunately, all of us had flexible employment where if we had to leave early on Friday to drive to a show, we could work that out with our bosses. But we did a lot of all-night drives to get back to work on Monday mornings.

Besides me, the band was Red Dorton on bass and background vocals. Robby Rigsbee was on rhythm and slide guitar. Josh Copeland was on lead and rhythm guitar and background vocals. Evan Wilons was on drums. We were a loud, proud Southern rock and blues band.

DOUBLE MEANING

Wanting to establish a new identity, we initially called ourselves the Zach Williams Band. But then an idea emerged to give the guys their own cool name, like Bob Seger and the Silver Bullet Band or Tom Petty and the Heartbreakers. One day we were all sitting around my parents' house, trying to come up with ideas. Our only criteria was that we wanted something that sounded very Southern. As uncool as this might sound to admit, my mom, who had been listening to us brainstorm and debate, spoke up and said, "Why don't y'all just call the band the Reformation?"

At first I wasn't sure what the word meant, but Mom explained that it was exactly what we were doing. We were *reforming*. We were creating a new band from an old one, working to get out of the dive bars, play original songs to have a real shot at the music business, and create a positive change for us all. But what Mom also knew was that the word was connected to the Reformation of the church led by Martin Luther in the 1500s.

So the discussion was over. Zach Williams and the Reformation was born. While we all thought the new name sounded cool, the big test was what our audience would think of it. But it didn't take long to see that the new name connected with our crowd. It's interesting to look back and see how these prophetic dynamics always seemed to be in play around me. No matter how far away I strayed or how deep I fell, the hand of God was always evident and sovereign in my life.

And I had no idea that I was on my way to experiencing my own reformation.

CHAPTER 5

MySpace, Her Space, Rock and a Hard Place

I can be so stubborn, caught up in my pride
Like I'm the only one who's strong enough to ever win the fight
I can do it on my own, never need a hand to hold
Yeah, I can be so selfish, holding on to what is mine
I can find a way to place the blame when my world ain't spinning right

With the new band formed, we had worked a deal to buy out all the equipment that the lead singer owned. I went to my parents' bank and got a loan to acquire my own gear as an equal partner. I bought our sound system—the mixing board and speakers. Every one of the guys was working hard to figure out their individual parts to the original songs. With each member of the band taking on a different support role on the business side, everyone felt like they deserved an equal take on the money. So after a lot of discussion, we agreed to create an equal five-way split on all income streams, including songwriting credits and royalties.

One of the inspirations for this decision was U2. In one interview, Bono talked about this dynamic within a group: "Let's start with the fact that it's the number one reason bands break up. Not musical differences, it's money differences. If you're the only one in the band who writes, remember the thing that will make your song famous is the band's playing of it. In U2 we decided to split things equally. I think it's at the top of the list of reasons we've lasted so long."[8] So with a handful of successful bands like U2 utilizing that strategy to try to maintain unity in the every-man-for-himself music business, we adopted that financial model right out of the gate.

While things were beginning to look up on the music front, my life was about to take another major turn. Her name was Crystal.

Scoot Over, Baby

Though both Crystal and I lived in the same small town of Jonesboro, Arkansas, hung around a lot of the same people, and went to many of the same parties, somehow we had never officially met. We could vaguely remember seeing each other out and about. This was right in the middle of the brief heyday of MySpace, so being the incredibly cool people we thought we were, both of us had accounts. I will forever have Crystal's profile picture locked into my memory. I have to confess I might have stalked her a bit on the platform after she first landed on my radar.

At the time, Crystal was dating a photographer who would shoot pictures at concerts, clubs, and other music events in the area. He would then post the photos on his website for people to buy. This was before Facebook became popular and way before everyone had amazing cameras on their phones to take pictures and post anything, anytime, all for free. So this guy had a good business going, making him a bit of a local celebrity. A big fish in a small pond, he was kind of a preppy, muscled-up jock. Crystal was the pretty girl on his arm everywhere he went, the trophy girlfriend for the cool guy. She was definitely the local "it girl" in town at that time.

Back when the guys were still known as Further Down and they were inviting me up to do a couple of songs, I remember seeing Crystal in the crowd and taking notice of her. But my opportunity to meet her came when I went to a club for a friend's birthday party. In the words of Hank Williams Jr., "all my rowdy friends" were there. I looked over and saw Crystal sitting in one of those half-circle booths with her boyfriend, but I wasn't too concerned about him. I thought, "Hey, there's that girl again. Here's my chance to try and get to know her." I decided right then and there to go over and make an impression.

I walked over and slid into the booth, right beside her. My plan was to accomplish two things: first, get her undivided attention, and two, provoke the boyfriend. No doubt, I was being obnoxious, loud, and downright rude. I ignored him and asked Crystal for her number. To my surprise, he got up and headed for the men's room, leaving me alone with her. When he finally came back, he just sat down on the other side of me, acting like he wasn't even paying attention to what I was doing.

Crystal was getting more and more uncomfortable with my aggressive flirting and asking for her number. She just kept pointing at the guy and saying, "You know, that's my boyfriend right there!" Every time, her warnings just caused me to turn up the heat and make some choice statements about him.

When I finally saw I was getting nowhere with Crystal, I decided to back off—for now. But I felt like I had accomplished my number one objective. She definitely knew who Zach Williams was now. But I realized my plan worked better than I thought when, soon after, she messaged me on MySpace and we traded phone numbers. *Boom!*

From Crystal

Although we didn't realize it until later, Zach and I had lived close to one another in Jonesboro for years. We had been hanging out in the same circles of people and going to the same parties in little houses but strangely, somehow, had never met. I remember later trying to figure out how we could possibly have missed each other. Finally, I asked him, "So, what did you look like? Did you look different then?" He answered, "I had like spikey, bleach-blond hair and wore all black with lots of chains." To which I said, "Well, that's why nothing happened! I was definitely not into *that* back then." I guess it just wasn't time for us to meet.

Zach's family lived about twenty minutes away from mine in Bono, Arkansas. In high school he dated a cheerleader from my school that I knew. She was a sweet girl. Of course, back then, Zach was a basketball jock, not a rocker. Even with all that history, we didn't officially meet until we were both twenty-nine years old, just one month apart in age. Here's the story of how we first met and talked. And I bet I give more details than he does.

My boyfriend at the time and I were at a club where a friend was having a birthday party. Suddenly, a tall, long-haired dude walked in. He had on a flannel shirt and bell-bottom jeans. The shirt was *definitely* a size too small for him. But I was like, "Who is *this*? Oh my gosh, I've never seen anything quite like *this* before!" He had my attention even before he walked over to where I was sitting.

Zach was so cocky when he sat down beside me. I was a bit shocked when the first thing he asked was, "Hey, you want to go out sometime? What's your phone number?" Then he proceeded to put his arm around me. I looked at him and was very clear: "That is my boyfriend right there." Zach made some comments about the guy that I won't repeat, but it was obvious Zach had no problem with riling him up.

So how did my boyfriend respond to the challenge? His reaction was nonchalant. He stood up and went to the bathroom! After Zach's advances didn't work with me, he finally got up and left. Later, my boyfriend told me in no uncertain terms to stay away from Zach. In fact, he warned me never to even speak to Zach again, threatening *me* instead of confronting *him*! But Zach is six-feet-six and a big, tough guy, so there is that.

When I got home, I went straight to my computer and got on MySpace to check out Zach's page. I remember looking at his picture and thinking, "Oh, hang on now. He's sexy." I was surprised to see we had been "friends" on the platform for about a year— more evidence of how much our friend circles had overlapped. The next night, I posted some corny message on Zach's page about his music. He confessed later about seeing my picture for the first time, telling me, "Your smile . . . I was enamored by it." (Okay, points for him on that line.)

Not long after that first meeting, my boyfriend and I were at another bar so he could take pictures of a band there. I was standing alone when, out of nowhere, Zach walked up. Obviously very high, he said, "I find you so attractive." (Yeah, just like that.) I immediately looked around to see where my boyfriend was and then told Zach, "We can't be talking like this!" But it was too late because the boyfriend saw us, causing yet another speech about never talking to Zach again. (But we all know human nature—when someone keeps telling us *not* to do something, what do we want to do? Yep, you got it.)

A couple of months went by, and I was supposed to go to a football game with my boyfriend, once again for him to take pictures. By now Zach and I had messaged on MySpace and traded phone numbers. He called and asked, "Hey, do you want to come over to my house tonight and hang out?" I was torn. Zach was wearing down my defenses. I couldn't escape my attraction to him. It was undeniable. Soon after I met him, I had a strange feeling I couldn't shake that I was going to marry the guy, definitely creating a wow moment for me in both attraction and chemistry.

So choosing between going to the football game with the boyfriend or hanging out with Zach, I chose

Zach. At his house, we started watching a documentary about some famous guitar player. At some point, I leaned over and kissed him. That sure broke the ice!

But, of course, my boyfriend was still in the mix and continued to try to talk me out of interacting with Zach. I abided by his wishes, and several months went by where Zach and I had very little interaction. But that all changed the day I showed up unannounced at the boyfriend's house to find obvious evidence he was cheating on me. Let's just say it was more than a kiss. Seeing all I needed to see, I walked out the door and called Zach. When he answered, I said, "Hey, this is Crystal. You want to go out sometime?" He told me that he and the band were in Memphis recording their first album. I could tell Zach was hesitant and acting a bit uninterested, which was surprising. He said he might call back later. I hung up, puzzled and disappointed.

According to him, before he made any commitment to getting together, he wanted to go to MySpace to check my relationship status. When he saw I had changed it to "single," he called back. Months before, he had decided he didn't want to create any more trouble between me and the boyfriend. Zach has never been a drama guy. He doesn't like to get mixed up in ongoing conflicts like that. But once he saw I really had ended it, our relationship began. We worked it out so I could come to Memphis while they were still working on the record.

As for the band, in 2008 we were ready to record our first album. Memphis was our closest and best option for a quality studio, and the guys had already recorded there before when they were Further Down. Their previous producer's girlfriend also produced, and we decided to go with her on our project, using a studio called Young Avenue Sound. Because I had recorded all my demos with me playing acoustic guitar and these were new songs to the guys, when we started recording in the studio, we had to work out all their parts as a band with the producer.

The entire time we were recording, we did a lot of drugs and alcohol. That's just what we thought we had to do to be a rock band. For our first session, we camped out in the studio for a week. There was a lounge above the control room where we stayed. The producer would get there by eight o'clock in the evening, and we would work until around four in the morning. We stayed drunk and high the entire time. We thought we had to be in that condition to be "creative." At the time, I didn't think about how I might sound, but when I listen to those songs today, I can hear how loose my vocals sound.

One of those first days working on the album, we had taken a short break when my cell rang. It was Crystal. She called to tell me she had broken up with the photographer. I was super excited at the news but tried hard to act cool. I wanted to be sure it was over. At first, I challenged her. "No, you didn't break up with him. Really? No way." Crystal answered, "Yep, trust me, it's definitely over." I put her off long enough to go check her MySpace status, but then called her back later to invite her to

Memphis. What could possibly be cooler than inviting a girl to a studio to watch you play and sing on a record, right? Granted, it's super boring once you get there, but the idea of it can sound romantic to someone who has never been before. When she arrived, the guys weren't particularly happy with me because none of the other wives or girlfriends ever came to the studio.

After Crystal and I started dating, I wrote a song about her, for her, called "Angel with a Broken Wing." We had already cut the song when, one day, the producer called me to say that the Black Crowes were going to be in Memphis and she knew Luther Dickinson. I knew all about Luther from his work with both North Mississippi Allstars and the Crowes. She said she could call and ask if Luther would come in and play slide guitar on "Angel." We were all over that idea because he had heavily influenced our own sound. When Luther agreed, we all made a special trip to the studio to hang with him for the day and listen to him cut his part of the song. As we knew it would, Luther's slide created such a cool feature.

Our first album, *Electric Revival*, was finally completed and released in 2009. Of the ten songs on the record, only one of my original thirty songs, "Without You," made its way onto that album. The other nine had been written since I started with the band.

Love Is a Battleground

Outside of working full-time for my dad and playing shows every weekend, Crystal and I became inseparable. Crystal had two children from a previous marriage. When I came into their lives, Julia was about to turn five years old and Gavin was almost ten. After spending plenty of time together and having a heart-to-heart about our relationship, I moved in with Crystal and her kids. By that point I was infatuated and totally in love with her. I quickly fell in love with her kids too. After living in the band house for two and a half years with a bunch of bachelors, I had some major adjustments to make to be around a woman and her young children.

Crystal and I, now both starting our thirties, had a lot of emotional baggage to deal with from past relationships. To deal with our issues, we were struggling in a lot of the same ways. While we had very different backgrounds, we had one huge thing in common: both our lives were a mess.

When I moved in with Crystal and the kids, trying to maintain my same old selfish habits, I would go in the bathroom, lock the door, open the window, and smoke pot. I was dumb to think that her kids wouldn't realize what was going on. Looking back at myself then, I was not a good dude. I remember constantly telling Crystal that I didn't and wouldn't change for her or anyone. I *was* a rocker and was going to *live* like a rocker.

From Crystal

Because Julia and Gavin loved Zach from the start, I wanted him to realize he needed to be a role model for them. But his response was always, "You knew who I was when you met me." I didn't expect him to raise them, but I did want him to be a good example of a man, at least on some level.

Early in our relationship, the band was doing a lot of pay-to-play shows to try to get the attention of labels or play-for-beer shows at clubs. It was really hard when he didn't make any money *and* he was getting drunk. Some nights Zach ended up owing hundreds of dollars to the bar by the time they finished playing. When he got smashed, he might announce from the stage, "Drinks for everyone on me!" Who at a bar doesn't love a band that buys everyone a drink? I had already lived the wild and crazy life, and especially with two kids, I was ready to settle down with some stability and peace. I quickly got sick of living the "rock and roll lifestyle."

That said, my draw to Zach was undeniable. It was pure love. I would sometimes jokingly think, "If we split up and he was with someone else, I'd have to kill her. And I don't want to go to jail." Even when we tried to split up, neither of us could leave. We were crazy in love.

A couple of months after we got together, some of Zach's friends and my friends went canoeing. Halfway down the river, Zach got really drunk. And then he became hard to manage. He kept tipping the canoe he was in, thinking it was funny. He wouldn't stop, so no one wanted to ride with him. Then he and one of the guys in the band started yelling, let's just say, some inappropriate things. Next, Zach was verbally abusive to me in front of everyone. I couldn't believe it. That was the first time I had seen or heard him be like that.

When we were finally back to the landing, I went to one of my girlfriends and cried my eyes out. And I am *not* a crier. But I felt like everything I thought about Zach had changed, and I was done. I wasn't going to put up with that behavior. By the time it got dark, he had started to sober up and was talking normal, so I went over to confront him. This became a significant moment for us because once I told him everything he had said *to* me and *about* me in front of everyone, he broke down weeping and apologizing. I will never forget looking at him and saying, "You know, Zach, for someone who always wants to be the life of the party, you have got to be the saddest person I've ever met. As messed up as my life is, yours is so much more."

That's the day I fully realized that Zach was one big wound. As we talked, I told him, "The reason you're doing all this stuff is because you're still beating yourself up for your past mistakes, all the way back to high school. I get it. You feel like you failed everyone in your life."

After that night, I kept my guard up, but it was too late. I was in love with him. So I was willing to take the risk to see where our relationship would go.

In every area of life, I was totally out of control. Partying way too hard, way too much. Drinking way too much. Using way too many drugs. Yet the entire time, now barely in my thirties, I kept working hard to keep my parents fooled. I wanted them to think there was no way I would be irresponsible, especially when it came to Crystal and her kids. Most days, I managed to make it to work and put in a full day, doing my share to help Dad on his jobs. But as soon as I left work, I turned back into the wild man again.

The biggest fights Crystal and I had weren't about my partying but about money. Although the two issues were connected, of course, the real problem was not having what we needed.

That dynamic is true for many couples. Being financially strapped is like a fuse constantly burning in the relationship. Then if any other stress or conflict is added, it sets off the bomb.

Yet, as the months passed, my behavior got worse. Crystal was getting a clear picture of what she had gotten herself into and was now convinced I would never change. She finally reached a point where she'd had enough and was ready to kick me out. But then something happened that we should have known was inevitable. Crystal told me she was pregnant with our first child.

With that surprise, as irresponsible and immature as I was, one thing I knew for certain—if we were going to have a baby together, I would do my very best to be a good dad. The sobering news caused us to try to quickly figure out how we could make life work, specifically our relationship. Suddenly, we had a huge motivation to get our act together. While Crystal may have been trying to figure out how she could live *with* me, now carrying our baby, she knew she didn't want to have to do this *without* me.

CHAPTER 6

STUMBLING INTO THE TRUTH

I spent so long
Living in the dark, living in the dark
I ran so fast
Until it fell apart, until it fell apart
Now I'm on my knees[9]

C rystal and I came to the mutual decision that we should do the best thing for our growing family and get married. So on May 6, 2009, we went to the local justice of the peace. With only the three of us present, Crystal and I became husband and wife. We didn't have the money to pay for any sort of ceremony, much less a reception, but we knew we were ready to be married. The most important thing to us wasn't the wedding but our marriage.

Then, four and a half months later, on September 21, our son Zephyn was born.

While our new baby boy was a huge blessing, unfortunately, marriage didn't change anything about our relationship. While the commitment to one another was a step in the right direction, it didn't affect our behavior. The same problems were there, except now with a newborn we were getting a lot less sleep. We still fought like cats and dogs, too often saying horrible things to each other. As the old saying goes, "Hurt people hurt people." I didn't think anything would or could ever change us.

We kept asking each other, "What do we have to do for our relationship to work?" But often, in frustration and anger, those questions would turn into harmful statements. For example, Crystal would say, "You're only with me because I have your son." So in an argument, I would use that fear against her: "Yeah, I'm only with you because you have my son." As sad and ashamed as I am to admit it, I once told her, "I can't stand you, but you have my kid, so I'm not going to leave." We talked about divorce a lot but never went past the threats. The battle of our wills was constant. But, strangely, the same passion that fueled our fights also seemed to be what held us together.

From Crystal

One time Zach and I were leaving a party to go home at about two o'clock in the morning. He was drunk, so I was driving. As we started down the road, he kept insisting he should take the wheel. I kept saying no, so he got mad at me. In all the back-and-forth confusion, I was going way too fast down the road. Suddenly, Zach yelled, "If you won't let me drive, then that's it . . . I'm jumping! I'm jumping out!" That's when he opened the passenger door. With it wide open and me not slowing down at all, I hollered back, "Well, go ahead! But I'm not stopping to go back and get you!"

By this point Zach was hanging out the door like a monkey. Because he's such a huge guy, he ended up bending my door back and ruining the hinges. It's amazing he didn't fall out.

His angels had to work a whole lot of overtime during those years. It was times like this that I felt like

---

I was in love with a Looney Tunes character. But, to be fair, when Zach was sober, which was much more than it sounds like, he was good and responsible and creative. These were the wonderful things I saw in him and loved about him, the things I knew just needed to somehow be brought front and center in his life. But I had no idea how that might ever happen.

ROCK STARS AND RISKY BUSINESS

After the band and I had finished our first record, we saw that Blackberry Smoke and the Delta Saints were doing a European tour, so we reached out to their agency. We sent them a CD of our new album, and they loved our songs and our sound. They signed us and booked a tour in Europe.

On March 8, 2010, almost a year after Crystal and I were married and Zephyn was six months old, the band flew out to start that tour. Our first show was in France on March 10. Our last night would be in Spain, with us playing fifteen shows in twenty days. This was the first time the band got a real taste of what it meant to be treated like rock stars. The promoter had us chauffeured everywhere we went, put us up in five-star hotels, and made reservations at nice restaurants. He also made sure there was a party everywhere we went.

For the entire tour, we were in an old Sprinter van. Our driver was a young Belgian man who was always doing as many drugs as we were. In the van, smoke was always thick in the air, and we stayed high. Most of the trips were only two to three hours long, a party on wheels. In Amsterdam, where it is legal, we bought a large stash of weed and hash. When we arrived at the border of Spain, we realized that what we had left of our drugs was illegal there, so one of the guys quickly ate what was left to get rid of it. Needless to say, for the next couple of days, he was a noodle. Yet another dangerous move.

The bar we played at in Belgium had some small apartments on the second floor where they told us we could stay. When the owner closed up that night after our show, he locked us in with full access to his liquor inventory. He had three craft beers that were rare, made by monks, and we drank from that tap all night long.

For our final show in Spain, we played with another US band on our agency's roster. The decision was made to stay in Granada and then leave the next day to drive through the night to get to France for the flight home—at least a twelve-hour trip. Being late winter, part of the route was through a mountainous region with snow and ice. Especially with the driver being high, that we never drove off a cliff or got into an accident was yet another sign of God's undeserved protection.

After the long drive, by the time we arrived at our hotel in France, we all felt deathly sick and had horrific headaches, which we just chalked up to the toll of our twenty-four-hour partying. Once I got to my room, I went straight to the shower. As the water hit my body and ran down to the drain, I noticed it was jet-black. That's when I realized I was covered in a thick soot. When I finally got it all washed off, I called the other guys and asked, "Have you taken a shower yet?" Every one of them answered that they'd had the same experience I did.

We decided to go out to the van with a roll of toilet paper. Wrapping our hands in a couple of layers of tissue, we wiped down several random spots all over the interior. Sure enough, *everything* was covered in the same black soot. Not only were we caked in it, but we had been breathing in and coating our lungs in this toxic mess for half a day! At the back of the van, we saw a piece of plywood cut to cover the floor, the same space where we had loaded our gear every night. We lifted that wood to discover a huge hole in the floorboard. Right below were the mufflers that had been constantly spewing diesel exhaust and carbon monoxide into the cab.

Most of our trips had been short, so we hadn't realized the problem. It's amazing we lived through that drive from Spain to France, as we were slowly being poisoned. From that final night's ride, I ended up with what felt like a bad case of bronchitis and completely lost my voice. That also explained why on our last show of the tour, I had lost my voice halfway through our set.

Because we had to be at the airport in Paris at four o'clock in the morning to fly home, we decided to stay up all night with the other band for one final night of partying. Someone had gotten a bottle of absinthe, which is derived from wormwood and usually around 60 to 70 percent alcohol. It is bitter and tastes similar to black licorice. Basically, we were out of our minds by the time we had to leave for the airport to head home.

We had gone from playing little bar gigs in the Southern

US to being treated like royalty abroad. In Europe, they love American rock music. The entire experience resulted in us thinking we had made it. We had finally hit the big time. We thought we were such a huge deal. But here's what we didn't yet understand: Every single dime the promoter had spent on us was being counted as expenses against our take of the ticket sales each night. At the end of the thirty days, we had made nothing. In fact, I'm surprised he didn't tell us we owed him money.

With four family members depending on me back home and not being at my construction job, I lost a month of wages. That was devastating for us financially when all I came home with was a horrible hangover from booze, drugs, and carbon monoxide poisoning. The constant craziness, coupled with the toxic van rides, made me sick for almost two weeks.

We returned from Europe in early April 2010. The agency had booked us on a USO tour in July to play for our troops in Guam and Japan. This time, there was real money to be made, the most money we had been offered—$25,000. Fortunately, we were able to convince our wives and girlfriends that this trip overseas would be very different from the Europe tour. Not only would we come home with money to pay bills, but we would also make enough to fund our second record.

But though we made more money, we partied the same as always. Every night of the USO tour, the American servicemen who were assigned to be our hosts would take us out to a bar. We got hammered with our troops for that entire week of shows. Like always, we thought it was our duty to act like rock stars. Looking back, I see how incredibly selfish I was in leaving my family and living like some kind of entitled bachelor, whether for a week or a month.

As soon as we were home and had divided up the money, we mapped out a plan for our second record.

WHISKEY AND WILDFIRES

The worse my substance abuse became, the more Crystal blamed the band. She wanted me to change so badly, and she saw the guys only as enablers of my behavior. Often one of them would bring me home after a show or practice, blasted out of my mind, and just drop me off, leaving Crystal to deal with me alone. Too many nights, I went from their party to her problem.

Whenever I got drunk on whiskey, I would come home mean—never physically abusive, but I had a really bad, mouthy attitude. Finally, one day, before I left to go rehearse with the band, Crystal made me promise I would stop. She said if I came home drunk on whiskey one more time, we were done. I told her I would just get high and agreed not to drink. But once I was at practice with the guys and a bottle came out, I threw that promise out the window.

From Crystal

Knowing the high level and potential of Zach's talent, I had a strong feeling the band wasn't right for him. When I tried to talk to him about going solo and hiring a backup band, he would get angry and say, "You just want me to quit music." To that, I would always say, "No, not at all. I just want you to be *successful* at it!" Eventually, I stopped going to their shows. Of course, I wanted to be supportive of my husband, but only in the right situation, in a healthy situation.

Late on the night that Zach had made me the promise about not drinking whiskey, I woke up from a sound sleep to realize he had come home drunk again. Once I heard his mouth and saw his mood, I knew it was whiskey. I was livid. As far as I was concerned, someone was leaving, and it was *not* going to be me. One hundred percent serious about my threat from earlier in the day, I told him to grab his stuff and get out. The argument started in the bedroom, went through the entire house, and ended up in the garage. We lived in an older home that had steps going from the house into the garage. With him being so much taller than me, I was standing on the third step to be able to look him right in the eye.

Zach popped off with exactly the kind of mean, rude remark that made me hate what the whiskey did to him. Now, I am not a violent person at all, but my patience and grace were running on empty by this point. Reacting to his insult, I balled up my fist and brought it up as fast and hard as I could to connect with his chin. You know the underwater footage on

Shark Week that shows a great white coming straight up from the depths at high speed to attack its prey on top of the water? That's a pretty good visual of my uppercut that night. (At least in my mind.)

When my punch connected, Zach's head shot back from the impact like whiplash in a car crash. He stumbled backward, hitting his head on the wall, making a dent in the sheetrock. (Since that's what he did for a living, I knew he could fix it later.) Even though my hand hurt a lot, I think my adrenaline was running so high that I didn't feel a thing. Zach quickly grabbed his face, thinking something was broken. He had one hand over his eye. He said I hit him so hard it must have fractured his eye socket.

What neither of us realized was that Robby, one of the band's guitar players, had started feeling guilty about dropping Zach off in such bad shape. He had turned around and come back, walking into the garage just in time to hear Zach's remark and see me throw the punch. He was standing there in shock with his mouth wide open. I looked at Robby and, quietly through clenched teeth, said, "I think you need to take him." He just nodded and walked over to help Zach stumble out of the garage to the car. I went back in the house, thinking that would go down as undoubtedly one of my greatest redneck moments.

After I finally went home late that night, I remember Crystal and I arguing about me being drunk and somehow ending up in the garage. That's when Crystal hit me so hard and fast that I did not see it coming. She had never done anything like that before, so I didn't expect that reaction. I also heard an odd clicking sound coming from somewhere in my face, and everything above my neck was in pain. Even if something was broken, I wasn't about to go to the doctor in this condition. That's when I realized Robby had shown back up to check on us. He walked into the garage and said, "Come on, Zach, get in the car."

After sobering up at his house, I knew I had deserved Crystal's reaction, knocking the fire out of me for whatever mean thing I had said to her. She was right about me and whiskey. For a few days, I laid low and we didn't speak. Once she finally agreed to talk, I apologized over and over, begging for her forgiveness once again. After Crystal said she would take me back, I went home with my tail tucked between my legs. Returning home, I knew something desperately needed to change because our marriage was hanging by a thread.

One ongoing argument was Crystal telling me that if the guys were really my brothers-in-arms and cared about me like I claimed, they would put a stop to the alcohol and drugs. But I just continued to insist that this was exactly what any decent rock and roll musician would be doing. Anytime the debate would start up, I would tell her, "You just want me to quit the one thing I really love! The thing I know I'm supposed to be doing!" That statement was a double whammy for Crystal. I was not only making her the bad guy but also backhandedly communicating that I loved the band more than I loved her. I would usually add, "You're the one person I'm trying to impress, and I need your approval more than anybody's. I don't care what anyone else thinks." Yet she stood her ground and kept making it clear that as long as I was behaving badly with the guys, she was *not* going to approve.

For these reasons, Crystal's view of the band had little to do with music. She saw it only as an excuse for getting drunk and getting high, all the while assuming that cheating on spouses and girlfriends was involved. I am happy and relieved to say I never gave in to that temptation. But with the substance abuse, anytime I tried to make peace and promise Crystal that I would not get messed up or come home in that condition again, I would blow it. That only led to an incredible level of distrust on every front.

If you've seen the movie *The Notebook* and the scenes with Noah and Allie in their younger years, Crystal and I were a lot like that. Whether loving or fighting, we were passionate in both. Our spark was always so strong that it was easy for us to start a wildfire.

THE CHOKE HOLD OF BAD CHOICES

By early 2011, because of the many years of living a horrible lifestyle and abusing my body, I started having severe problems with gastroesophageal reflux disease, commonly known as acid reflux. I had developed a stricture so bad that my throat closed up to the point I could barely swallow, much less sing. I couldn't eat anything solid. During a trip to the emergency room, a doctor went in and dilated my throat, stretching it back out. But while the scope was in there, he discovered I was in the early stages of Barrett's esophagus, a condition where the lining of the swallowing tube that connects the mouth to the stomach becomes damaged, causing it to thicken and inflame. They also found some precancerous cells. My body was giving me a wake-up call.

While such a condition isn't necessarily brought on from alcohol abuse, my lifestyle had certainly made mine worse. When you take a bottle of whiskey and drink it like it's a can of soda, one way or another, that level of excess is going to eventually catch up with you. The amount of acid created by and coming back up from my stomach was horrible. My doctor told me I needed to be on medication and also had to radically alter my diet. He let me know that if I didn't make the necessary changes, I would develop esophageal cancer. For a guy who's a lead singer for a living, this was a real threat in several ways.

After I heard the doctor's stern warning, I went to talk to the band. They saw how serious I was as I explained, "Hey, for my health, I need to step away for a bit. I have to take a break." Me being out of commission for even a short time was not the news they wanted to hear. It didn't go over well. For a while, they tried to lock me out of the bank accounts, acting like they were going to move on and do the band without me.

So I finally caved to their desires and kept going, ignoring my doctor's warnings.

The fears for my health and the band's lack of support, coupled with the volatility in my relationship with Crystal at the time, sent me into another depression. In keeping with my pattern when facing a crossroads, I chose the wrong direction. I started living harder than ever. For the next year, I dove even deeper into the dark world of drugs and alcohol. I told myself, "Well, this is it. I'm living hard and dying young like many of my rock star heroes have done—Hendrix, Janis, Jim Morrison, and Kurt Cobain. I'm only a few years past being a candidate in the 27 Club of rock and roll. If that's my fate too, then so be it."

I reached the point where I was embarrassing myself, making it harder and harder to cover my tracks from all the stupid stuff I was doing. One night before leaving the next day to go play shows for the weekend, a bunch of us guys went out to party. We decided it would be funny to play "Fight Club" in the parking lot of a bar, seeing who could get hit in the face the hardest and walk away. We were all swapping licks and taking hard shots to see who could keep standing, laughing at each other after every punch.

When we got back to our house, the guys and I kept going. I ended up putting my hand through our garage window. When I pulled it out of the broken glass, blood was squirting everywhere. The exposed tendon that goes from my pinky to my elbow looked like a rubber band. They took me to the emergency room, where a doctor sewed me up, but from that night on, I haven't been able to lift my little finger. It's completely dead from the damaged tendon. But, thank God, I can still play guitar.

Once again, I didn't want my parents to know the truth about my bandaged hand. I made up a story about getting jumped in an alley and cut with a beer bottle. I convinced them again that none of it was my fault. From the wild stories I made up as a kid to circumstances like this as a grown man, the lying went on for far too long.

When patterns of dysfunction become so deeply ingrained in our hearts, it's like dried-out tire ruts on a once-muddy road. You can just drop the wheels in, take your hand off the steering wheel, and let the grooves take over.

From Crystal

When I was growing up, my family was very dysfunctional. In short, I felt like there was no love in our house. So watching Zach's family deal with him, I loved it on one hand but hated it on the other. I wanted to experience what they had, but I didn't understand it. I usually saw their acceptance only as enabling him, but I could also see it as their expression of God's grace to their son.

Once when Zach was at the hospital for one of his injuries, his mom and I were in the waiting room.

I decided it was time to be brutally honest with her about his lies. I spilled my guts and ended with, "I'm telling you this because you both need to realize that Zach has a problem, and if we don't come together to get him some help, he's going to die." I felt like I had to confront the truth because I loved him. I cared about him. And I knew they did too.

HABITS, HALF-TRUTHS, AND A HAIL MARY

On one trip to play at a radio station in Poplar Bluff, Missouri, the guys wanted to stop at a "certain club" they knew about. I had given Crystal my word that I wouldn't go to places like that. Because Robby and I didn't want to go but also didn't want to create a rift, we said we would just stay in the van and wait on the other guys. When we got home, Crystal had spoken to one of the other wives about their suspicions and asked me if I had gone there. I said no. By staying in the van, I felt like I was being honest without throwing anyone under the bus (or van, in our case).

When one of the other guys finally confessed to his girlfriend where we had stopped, that made it look like I had lied to Crystal. Even though they worked hard to tell the ladies that Robby and I didn't go in, the story was hard to believe, as in, "Oh, so you waited in the van for two hours while everyone else went in, huh?" Because I had tried to do the right thing for once, I got so mad when Crystal wouldn't believe me that

I went outside and started kicking the cedar post that held up one of the corners of our carport. I kicked it so hard that I fractured my knee. The next day at work, the lie I came up with for Dad was that I had stepped off the back of the band trailer and turned my knee. Situation after situation, it was getting harder to cover my tracks. To believe everything that I said happened to me, you would have to assume I was the clumsiest, most accident-prone guy on the planet.

With life literally out of control, I reached the point of being miserable twenty-four seven, and it was nobody's fault but mine. I couldn't seem to figure out how to step up and be a man. During those crazy years, some nights I would get drunk and know better than to go home and put Crystal through another scene. Instead, I would go to my parents' house, and they would make coffee to try to sober me up. They were watching all this happen but still wanted to believe it wasn't as bad as it looked.

My constant inward struggle was wondering how I could make everyone I loved happy. I was in a "band marriage" with four other guys and an actual marriage with Crystal. I could go play music with the band and not fight, then come home to my wife and fight. While playing music was always an escape, I knew the guys were not thinking about my well-being and my family. I could see that Crystal was looking out for my best interest as a man, a husband, and a dad. I had two things I loved, and I could never reconcile the two. I couldn't and didn't want to give up my family. But if I gave up music, I thought I would never have the opportunity again.

From Crystal

One time when Zach had come home horribly drunk early in the morning, I'd had enough and called his parents. Zach's dad came to the house. He is one of the sweetest men I have ever known. He never yells. He's just not that guy. He was crying and told Zach he needed to accept Jesus, that where he was headed was not the life God had for him. Zach went into his excuse about being a rock star and how living this lifestyle was what he was supposed to do. I responded with, "That doesn't make any sense. Who wants you to be an alcoholic and a drug addict? Is that *really* what a rock star is? You're not going to make it if you keep living like this!" I know that day was a big eye-opener for Zach's dad, and it was hard for us all.

I remember one particular morning when Dad came over. Still drunk from the night before, I stumbled down our stairs and fell. As he sat on the couch watching me, Dad started to cry. Then, through his tears, he prayed out loud for me. But as soon as he went out the front door to leave, I walked outside on the back porch and lit up a joint. My heart was moving past just hardening; I was becoming calloused.

Eventually, my parents realized they couldn't deny my issues any longer. Crystal had tried hard to help them understand, and they finally faced the truth. Dad and Mom started regularly coming over to our house to pray for me and Crystal. They would also invite us to church. But that was one place I wasn't about to walk into, to be judged by everyone. I could feel that way about myself just fine without anyone's help.

During Dad's visits, he would always tell Crystal and me that God had big plans for us. Sometimes, out of desperation and often frustration, I would ask him, "Well, then why can't I see it?" Dad would always answer, "Because, son, if He were to show you the plan for your life right now, it would blow your mind. You wouldn't be able to handle it." In those moments, I was too lost to see the truth. I didn't believe anything good could possibly come out of my life. What I couldn't see at the time was that, in his younger days, Dad had managed to get through to the other side and was looking at life through his relationship with Jesus. He could see in his faith what I couldn't see in my fear. Mom and Dad had walked through something similar in their first years of marriage and had come out much better. But Crystal and I were still stuck on the far shoreline.

I was living so differently than how I had been raised. When Dad realized he was going the wrong way, he humbled himself and straightened up. But I kept going further in the wrong direction. Still, I knew enough to see that my choices were wrong. I knew better. That's why the guilt and shame were piling up higher and higher and smothering me. I knew there had to be more to life than what I was experiencing. I knew a lot about heaven, but my life felt more like hell. But even in the darkness, a tiny glimmer of light can still be seen. In my heart, I hoped there could still be some kind of answer for me, some way that everything that was going so wrong could be turned around and made right.

Even though I was still angry with the guys for their response to my health scare, we straightened things out enough to take the money we had saved from the USO tour and go to Nashville for a week to record our second album at Black River Studio. The first record had taken almost a year of back-and-forth to Memphis to finish, but we decided to knock out this second project much quicker. *A Southern Offering* was released in April 2011. The lyrics reflect the depth of my struggles with life and my desperate search for truth. When I listen to those songs today, I hear a man crying for help.

Two things were now constantly brewing in the back of my mind. First, I had to figure out a way to make some actual changes in my life. I knew if I didn't, I would lose my family, which was about to expand to six. Second, I was starting to question my place in the band and wondered how this chapter in my music career might end.

In a repeat scenario from the first record, right around the release of the new album, our agency worked on booking another tour in Europe for the summer of 2012. Early that year, between the craziness with Crystal and me, the band, and my bad behavior, she became pregnant with our daughter.

With only a couple of months left before we were to leave for Europe, one night on the road, the band stayed at a hotel in

Cape Girardeau, Missouri. Robby and I were in a double room together late on a Friday night. Out of the blue he said, "Hey, I wanted to tell you that I'm catching a ride home tomorrow night after the show. I need to be back for Sunday morning. I'm playing at a church service that my wife and I have been going to for a few weeks now."

I did *not* see that coming. I immediately thought, "Church! You're going to go from playing a club on Saturday night to playing in church on Sunday morning? Can you even do that? Is that allowed?" But instead I responded with, "What? Really? . . . Wow." Robby explained: "Yeah, we got this card in the mail a while back about a new church service, and we decided to try it out. After a couple of weeks of being there and getting to know some of the people, they invited me to play with the worship band." I think my response to Robby was surprising to us both. Something in me pushed past all the bad history and personal bias as I blurted out, "Dude, I wanna go too!"

When I got home from playing shows that weekend, I told Crystal about my conversation with Robby. She was surprised too when I told her I wanted us to go with them to visit this church. Because she was ready to try almost anything at this point, Crystal quickly agreed. Beyond ready for a major life change, she was so done and so sick of everything. She was over my rock and roll lifestyle and ready to do whatever it took to get my life straightened out. Crystal knew that the band and being on the road was going to take me down sooner rather than later. She saw it coming like the headlights of a freight train.

From Crystal

Robby was always a compassionate, kind man, so when he started going to church, that was a game changer. He was never the troublemaker. Being the most responsible of them all, he always tried to keep the band organized and handle the money carefully. That's why I was so glad Zach was eventually the most drawn to Robby. He told Zach that he was looking for more, trying to find more meaning in life. He felt like his answer to that search was God. The conversation that night in the hotel room on the road was the beginning of answered prayers for us.

The next weekend, the Sunday after Easter 2012, Robby and I came home late Saturday night after a show. As planned, Crystal and I got up early and went to church with them. Not sure how I would feel, I was pleasantly surprised that I didn't have all the toxic and negative emotions I felt when my parents invited us to church. I remember walking in, looking around, and thinking, "This is exactly where I'm supposed to be." Such a strange experience. Maybe it had something to do with me choosing it for myself and not feeling like anyone was trying to guilt or coerce me.

When a person struggles with drugs and alcohol and someone is telling him or her to stop, that never seems to work. But when the person decides they've finally had enough, the door to change can be unlocked. What caused me to be open to this church was knowing I hadn't been on "the prayer list" for the past ten years. I couldn't be judged before I ever set foot in the door. Here, no one knew my history, and that was something I was ready to experience. A clean slate. A fresh start. A new day.

I had the odd sense that I'd finally found a home.

CHAPTER 7

BAR STOOLS AND CHURCH PEWS

Are you lost and wanna be found?

Are there shackles on your feet that weigh you down?

Are you scared there's no way out?

Are you sick and tired of falling on the ground?[10]

Late the night before, I had been playing in a club full of people who wanted only to party and find love or lust or something as close to either as they could get. Knowing our plan to go to church on Sunday morning, I had made sure I stayed sober to be as ready as I possibly could. It was going to be weird to trade bar stools for church pews, blues for praise, and drunks yelling "Freebird!" for believers shouting "Amen!" Other than the few times I caved to my parents' invitations, I hadn't been to church in over a decade, so I felt a strange combination of being terrified and excited. But here I was, about to walk into my first shot at trying to find a real answer for all the personal battles I'd fought for far too long.

This particular service at the church was held in a small room to be more intimate, but the building itself was massive. This was a Southern Baptist megachurch that everybody in the area jokingly called "Six Flags Over Jesus" because of the size of the campus and the number of activities held there every week. At that time, they had about two thousand people at each of their services. The parking lot on Sunday morning looked like the mall at Christmastime. But this new service where we went had only a couple hundred people. The goal of the church staff was to offer an alternative worship experience for people who weren't accustomed to coming to church—the "unchurched," as they call them.

Before the service started, people were coming up and loving on us—smiling, welcoming, shaking hands, hugging, introducing themselves, saying, "We're so glad you're here." The big surprise was that they all sounded like they meant it! A few of the folks knew who Robby and I were because of the local popularity of the band. Yet there seemed to be no judgment from anyone on how we looked or what we did for a living. No one was looking us up and down and walking away or acting like we were invisible. No "Why are *you* here?" vibes at all. Nothing felt stuffy or religious or formal.

Not only did I survive the hour, but Crystal and I enjoyed the experience of being in church together. We knew we would be coming back the next Sunday. We also found out there was a five o'clock service on Sunday afternoons, which was perfect for us after getting home from our weekend road schedule.

The following Friday, while the band was driving to a show in Little Rock, Robby told all the guys that he was getting baptized at the church on Sunday. They quickly started kidding around and giving him a hard time. But after those remarks settled down, I smiled and encouraged him. "Dude, that's so awesome!" I'm sure my response was both surprising and confusing to them. But I think something about Robby being a step ahead of me in the whole experience caused me to cheer him on and keep moving forward, right behind him in this new journey. That way, I could see what was next, how it went for him, and how I felt about it all.

For the next few Sundays, the "something" I had wondered for so long if it existed and hoped for began to be revealed. The elusive answer suddenly seemed like it had been there all along. To repeat, thank God, I was never addicted to any of the many substances I had abused since I was a teenager. Somehow I was always able to turn it on and off at will. Granted, whenever I flipped the switch on, it was like a fire hose. Once Crystal and I started going to church and I realized there was another life available to me, I quit partying.

Alcohol and drugs had been a habit for too long. While I could live without them, up until this point, I had just chosen not to. My indulgence was always about personal medication. The best way I can describe my behavior was bingeing. As I've said, my competitive nature also kicked in and made me want to go harder than anyone else in the room. I worked a regular job at least four days a week and then played "rock star" every weekend. This strange dual identity made me not want to deal with the realities of my life. I wanted to stay comfortably numb. While I don't think I was ever in a state to need to check in to rehab, now I had finally connected with something I had never been able to find—a real reason to stop and something good to replace it with, which was to save my life and my family with the help of a new community of support. In just a few short weeks, I was in a much healthier place and, thankfully, Crystal and I were doing better than we ever had before.

From Crystal

When Zach said he was finally ready to make any sort
of change, that he would go to church where Robby
was going, I was beyond willing to try anything. By
that point, I was broken. Growing up, my family
had considered themselves to be spiritual but not
Christian. We never talked about God in our home.
We didn't believe in Jesus as Lord. With all the
dysfunction, when I became an adult, I claimed to be
an atheist. But, in reality, it was more that I turned my
back on God, not that I didn't believe in Him. After
all, you don't try so hard to ignore Someone that you
don't believe exists. In college, I even got on board with
trying to disprove the Bible by minoring in biblical
studies. I wanted to know more so I could prove it was
false. By the time I met Zach, I felt like I was willing
to pay the consequences for turning my back on God,
whatever they might be. For a long time, I stopped
caring about any sort of faith.

Early on, after a while of Zach and I partying
together at his shows, I reached the point where
I would walk into a club or bar and felt like I was
witnessing death. I looked around and had trouble
seeing a soul in anyone there. My mind and my heart

were starting to change. God was working on me. I had no desire to judge anyone, I just clearly saw there was no life in *that* life.

When I was ten years old, we lived on a street with a Baptist church at the end of the block. I started walking there on Sundays by myself. I met the pastor and got to know the other kids. They took me with them to a Billy Graham revival. I remember hearing the gospel and thinking how I wanted this Jesus he was talking about. I remember being on my knees. I was broken. I didn't understand what I was feeling, but I knew I wanted more of whatever was present in that place. Unfortunately, right after that, things got really bad in our house and that's when I was introduced to drugs. Now I can look back and know that the Enemy was working hard to keep me from turning my life over to Christ. Regardless of my volatile background, when I had my own kids, I knew I wanted them to have the opportunity to embrace faith in a way I never got to experience.

The Sunday morning that Zach and I first walked into church together, as soon as the pastor started teaching, he spoke life into us. We both knew it. We could feel it. Together, we agreed, "This is it for us." We were ready for the Truth after many years of lies.

Welcome to Self-Sabotage

The more our life improved as a family, the more I tried to figure out an exit from the band. By now, the European tour was right around the corner, and I was battling the decision within my own heart, constantly thinking, "How do I leave for Europe now after I've been in church for only a month? After being there for just a few weeks, I'm starting to feel much better. How can I leave? What will happen if I do?" I knew how easily I could get off track if I stepped far outside this new life I was experiencing. I needed more time to get stronger. So as the days went by and the tour got closer, I kept telling Crystal that I didn't feel like I should go.

Finally, I decided I had to talk to the band. I knew that confessing how close I was to not going at all would freak them out, so I took a different approach by asking some questions about the tour. Plus, there were some things I needed to know for the sake of my growing family. The next time we were all together, I opened up. "You guys know that, after we paid all the expenses, the first tour we did in Europe didn't make *any* money. This time, with three kids and one on the way, I'm going to have to miss a month's worth of work with my dad. I need to know I'm getting paid enough to make going over there for that long worthwhile." Then I asked for specifics. "So what exactly do the numbers look like this time around? What can we actually bring home?"

I knew full well that the discussion was pointless. The shows were booked. Tickets had been sold. Flights and hotels were secured. Instruments, gear, and production were reserved. Transportation around Europe was ready to go. The band had everything on the line. The guys worked hard to assure me that this time was going to be different. This trip would be more than worth the time away.

Feeling like I had no choice, knowing we were locked in, I worked hard to ignore the increasingly loud voice of reason telling me I didn't need to leave on this trip. Knowing the guys would party like always, I tried to convince myself that I could go to Europe for a month and stay sober. I had to somehow come up with the willpower to say no the entire time, no matter what went on around me. Accepting my fate, I played this speech on repeat in my head: "Just go over there and do your job. Play the shows, stay out of trouble, enjoy the sights, collect the paycheck, come home, and walk right back into where you left off. But whatever you do, do not go backward."

But just like Jesus said, "The spirit is willing, but the flesh is weak" (Matthew 26:41 NIV). On May 25, 2012, within a few hours of our plane landing in Barcelona, the drinking started. We went to an outdoor restaurant with tables lined down the street. The food was incredible, and we went through way too many bottles of wine. I jumped right back into the deep end. The party had started back up.

For a musician or crew member on the road, it's easy to create a Jekyll and Hyde lifestyle: responsible family man and community member at home, wild man on the road. The two extreme environments can create a weird schizophrenia-type existence, a "double-minded" and "unstable" man, as James said (James 1:8 NIV). All you have to do is read some of the many biographies of famous touring artists in modern music to hear about this strange dynamic that any of us as sinners can easily fall into.

You also see it often with people who travel a lot for their jobs. Being bored and lonely in a city where you don't know anyone and having way too much time on your hands can be trouble. For musicians, whether we're playing arenas or dive bars doesn't really make any difference. The common thread is being outside your support system with no real accountability. Total strangers have high expectations of you but also sing your praises. Fame on *any* level for any reason can become a dangerous, self-destructive beast that consumes you. I'm not offering this as an excuse or rationale for anyone, just stating the facts. To survive, you have to have strategies in place *before* you leave.

I hadn't been in Europe long when, one night back home, Crystal hosted an in-home party with a woman selling a line of beauty products. Crystal had a living room full of ladies, including my mom. Blasted out of my mind, for some reason I decided it would be a good time to call my wife. The time zone difference, as well as our different schedules, had made it hard to find a good time to talk. Seeing it was me calling, Crystal grabbed her phone and stepped outside to answer. Not only was I slurring incoherently, but my belligerent tone was clear. Crystal knew immediately what that meant—the "new Zach" hadn't lasted long in Europe. She was extremely hurt and disappointed. I had let her down again.

Crystal walked right back into the house, got my mom's attention, and motioned for her to come outside. While I was yelling and carrying on, Crystal put me on speaker for my mother to hear it all firsthand. After a couple of minutes, my now hurt and angry mom tried to interrupt me but eventually gave up. At some point, they hung up on me.

Mom had always been the one person to give me the benefit of the doubt and try to come up with some reason why things with me weren't as bad as they appeared. That night was her wake-up call and last straw, all in one moment. Even a loving Christian mom has limits.

The next day when I woke up, my hangover was horrific. Coming out of my stupor, I was hit with hazy memories of being on the phone with Crystal *and* Mom. I realized they had both heard enough. So here I was in the worst place of my life. I had officially hit bottom and had nowhere to look but up.

The entire day, I was terribly sick—physically, emotionally, mentally, and spiritually. Having to leave for our next show, I sprawled on the floorboard of the Sprinter van, tucking myself under one of the seats as far as my six-foot-six frame would allow. I couldn't even lift my head. At some point during the drive, the van had a blowout. I was so messed up that I didn't notice when we pulled to the side of the road and all the guys got out. When I finally woke up, I was soaked in sweat because it had to be over a hundred degrees in that van with no AC. I managed to look out to see everyone sitting under a tree, waiting on road service to come change the tire.

From Crystal

After our family started going to church, life was slowly changing for the better. With Zach two weeks away from going to Europe, I kept thinking, "Okay, it's only been a few weeks. Will he be able to hold it together there? I just don't think he's strong enough yet. It's way too soon to go back into that much temptation."

Pregnant with our daughter, I called Zach's mom and asked to come over to speak with her. After we sat down together, I got straight to the point. "Look, if Zach gets over there and starts partying with the guys, if he comes back from Europe worse this time, I need you to know I'll have to walk away, for me and the kids' sake. I just don't want you to be surprised if I have to do that."

I could tell what I was saying was very hard for her to hear and difficult to process. After all, I was talking about her only son and her grandbabies. But my concerns were real, and I didn't want to appear impulsive, should my hand be forced. While I knew I had reached my limit with Zach's partying with the band, I had now also tasted what life could be like for us moving forward, if he stayed with what we had been experiencing since going to church.

A week or so after Zach went to Europe, I had a party in our home for a lady selling beauty products. While everyone was visiting, Zach called. With the huge time zone difference, I felt like I needed to answer. When I did, I couldn't understand what he was saying. He made no sense. As I tried to deal with him, he grew louder and stronger with me. Realizing his horrible state, I went in and asked his mom to join me outside. I told her, "I just want you to hear what I've had to deal with these past few years." Then I put Zach on speaker. We both stood there listening to him go on in his drunken rant. His mom tried to interrupt and talk to him. "Zach, what is going on? What is wrong with you? I can't believe you're doing this! Now I see what Crystal has had to deal with." As hard as it was on her, she realized the truth. As a mom who loves her kids deeply, I fully understood the pain this harsh reality was for her.

Zach's mom was upset and heartbroken. After she got home that night, she sent him a message. Because it was hard to reach him by phone, she decided to write out her feelings. Her words to him were clear. She told him in no uncertain terms how deeply disappointed and sad she was. Her words hit Zach hard, but he needed to hear them.

Once we were back on the road and arrived at our hotel where I was alone and coherent, the reality of everything that had happened the day before started to set in. Then I saw I had a message from my mom. Knowing what it would be about, I opened and read it right away.

Mom had already been messaging me regularly. Her first message, on May 30, *before* the phone call, read, "Hope all is well on the tour. Just hoping and praying you aren't getting a taste for that liquor again. Stay true to yourself and your family. Love you. You've conquered this in the past. Don't make it something you have to wrestle with again. Be strong."

Her message the next day, May 31 at 9:25 p.m., *after* the call, read, "Apparently you aren't as strong as I thought! I try to encourage Crystal to trust you, but it seems you aren't trustworthy! I thought you cared more for your family, but it seems you only care about yourself. I'm really disappointed that you got drunk again. Thought you had gotten past that. As the pastor told you, 'You can't have the rock star mentality and stay healthy.' Hopefully, you won't give Crystal anything else to be upset about for the rest of the trip."

When I finished reading her words of disappointment about me and her alliance with Crystal, I felt like I was drowning in guilt and shame. I had the punched-in-the-gut feeling you get when you know you've blown it so badly that you could finally be at the point of no return. The two people I loved most had stood together in my backyard, hearing me at the lowest moment of my life. I had let Crystal down. I had let my parents down. And I had let myself down. And just as I was starting to figure out that God really did love me, I had turned my back on Him again. My fears that I couldn't do this trip without going backward had proven true, my failure now obvious to us all.

On June 1 at 4:01 a.m., I sent Mom a message that read, "All I can say is I'm sorry. I talked to Crystal and told her I only have myself to blame. It's just my fault. I'm sorry."

Later that day, Mom sent back a response. "I hope you'll be strong enough for the rest of the trip to say no when tempted. If a so-called buddy tries to entice you, then he is not much of a friend. Crystal loves you, but one of her biggest fears is that you'll begin drinking again. If you can't lay that down, you'll probably lose some important things in your life. And like I told you a year or so ago, God is not going to bless you with success in that band because He knows where it's going to take you and He knows that you can't handle it. Hopefully, Crystal will get over this, but it's like the guy who beats his wife— sorry doesn't mean much after you've heard it enough. It still takes action. Still love you though. Zephyn and I looked at your pics on Facebook, and he needs you to come home soon. It's hard for him to understand why you're gone. Keep him in your thoughts, and it will help you stay strong. Get over this and move on."

Lying in a hotel room somewhere in Europe, feeling sick and tired, alone and isolated from everyone, I decided to pray. This was not the 9-1-1 kind of prayers I had said before. This time was different. This was desperation. This was my white-flag moment of finally giving up the fight. Falling to my knees, I pleaded, "God, if you're real . . . if you're Who You say You are . . . if You can show me somehow that You're there, then I'll walk away from all of this and never look back."

Moment of Truth

That's where and when and how my real turnaround began.

A radical change in my life started to take root.

Two days later, with me sobered up and all my senses sharp and alert, we were in a Sprinter van driving across Spain. I was reading Gregg Allman's memoir, *My Cross to Bear*. In the book, Gregg talks about all the years he struggled with substance abuse while dealing with fame and life on the road in a rock and roll band. No coincidence on *that* timing. John Mayer had just released his *Born and Raised* album, a mature, more laid-back acoustic record with songs that spoke right to me, like "The Age of Worry," "Love Is a Verb," and "If I Ever Get Around to Living." I had my headphones on, listening intently and reading Gregg's book at the same time. Taking inventory of everything I was feeling about my life, I struggled most with this question: "Why can't I just walk away from these things that keep hurting me?"

That night, on our eight-hour drive to the next show, all the guys were sound asleep. Our German driver, who spoke very little English, was at his post, quiet and focused. I pulled off my headphones, put down the book, and stared out the window. I had an odd feeling I needed to sit in the stillness and listen with my heart.

Out of my peripheral vision, I noticed the driver reach over and start to scan through the radio. For some reason, he stopped on an English-speaking station. The lyrics to the song that was playing were words I wasn't used to hearing, like "bound up," "prisoner," "unworthy," "shame and regret." But then I heard others, like "set me free," "wipe away," and "not who I used to be." They all described exactly where I was and where I desperately wanted to be. I felt like the song was *about* me and *to* me.

Amazed, I had no idea who the artist was or why they were singing about *my* life. The song turned out to be Big Daddy Weave's "Redeemed."

After staying on the station just long enough for me to hear the message, the driver hit the button again and moved on. But I had heard exactly what God wanted me to hear: a short, powerful sermon in a song. I realized He was answering my "show me You're real" prayer. How in the world does a German van driver who doesn't speak English stop to listen to an American song on a Christian radio station in the middle of Spain? No matter what your spiritual paradigm might be, that one is hard to explain outside of it being miraculous. Funny how when you pray a prayer like I did in that hotel room, your logical self disbelieves that anything will actually happen, even though in your heart you hope it will. I think that's what makes an answer that you can't deny so much more powerful.

I grabbed my phone to search for the song by typing in all the lyrics I could recall. When we got to our hotel, I listened to "Redeemed" on repeat, over and over and over again, allowing the words to sink in to my heart. Then I began to sing them for myself. As the truth of the song pierced my soul, I started to connect with the gospel message that I had missed for all those years. While I still had a lot of fear and believed too many lies,

I was beginning to glimpse who God is and the truth of how He actually sees me.

I knew that even with all the damage I had done to our marriage, I had to call Crystal to tell her what was happening. Thank God she answered. I quickly tried to explain what I had prayed and then how I had taken off my headphones just in time to hear "Redeemed" on the radio. Then all I could do was just keep asking for her forgiveness through my tears. (At that point I had no idea about the talk she'd had with my mom before I left for Europe.) Having heard my desperate promises before, she did *not* want to hear any more. I tried hard to explain that *this time* was different. This wasn't just me aiming to "try harder," to do it in my own strength. Something was happening *in me* that was somehow coming from *outside of me*.

Over the phone I pleaded, "No, no, Crystal, you don't understand. I'm serious this time. I'm done!"

As hard as I was trying to convince her, she was challenging me right back.

"Yeah, well, Zach, you're going to have to prove it to me. Because I don't believe you."

Then I said the words that just a few months before I had sworn I would never speak, a promise that Crystal certainly never thought she would hear.

"Crystal, when I get home, I'm quitting the band."

We both went silent. After a long pause, I continued, "Please don't say anything to the other wives because if it gets back to the guys while we're here, I will never hear the end of it for the rest of this tour."

Crystal heard the sincerity in my voice but still was not convinced. She was asking herself, "Is this for real, or is he so desperate for forgiveness that he'll promise me anything?"

Over the next several days, I was grateful that the change of heart and my feelings of repentance stayed strong. I would go to sleep and wake up with the same conviction the next day. Something new was happening in me that I had never experienced before. I called Crystal every day and repeated my promise to her: "I'm sober and I'm serious. When I get home, I'm done." I wanted her to know I was committed to staying true to what I said.

From Crystal

One day while in the shower—*after* the drunken phone call that Zach's mom was in on but *before* he called me about his encounter with and decision to follow Jesus—I replayed in my mind how Zach's parents had dealt with everything he had done over the years. I began to realize how much forgiveness and grace they had shown him. I became emotional, praying out loud, "God, this makes no sense. I just don't understand. Why do they *keep* forgiving him?" As soon as I asked the question, I felt like He spoke to me in my spirit, saying, "Crystal, I'm here for you. I've always been here with you. I've always been your Father. When no one else was there, I was."

> I had my aha moment with God around the time
> Zach had his. Suddenly, I felt like the water rushing
> over me from the shower was washing away all the
> years of pain.

COMING HOME

I couldn't wait for the tour to be over and to get home. At the
point of my revelation, we were about halfway into the tour.
Every day in Europe, while the guys continued their usual
partying, I worked hard to stay clean and sober. Another part of
my "show me You're real" prayer was to have the strength to keep
saying no day in and day out, even if that meant being alone.

On our last night in Europe, somehow I was given my own
room. I remember lying in bed, not being able to sleep. In my
thoughts, I rehearsed what I would say to Crystal when I got
home, the breakup talk with the band, and my discussion with
Dad to let him know I was ready to be full-time *and* focused. No
more Fridays off, no more late Monday mornings, and no more
getting high on the job. I was planning out my new life that
would begin the second I got back.

After sixteen shows in Europe, on June 10, 2012, we finally
arrived back in the US and I walked in the door of our home.
I dropped my bags and went straight to Crystal, apologizing
and crying. I looked her in the eye and repeated everything I
had been telling her on the phone. "I'm so sorry. None of that
old stuff is ever going to happen again. We're going to church

this Sunday. We *are* going to start a brand-new life. I'm done." She heard me out and was supportive, but I knew I had to give her real proof over time so she could see for herself. And I couldn't—and didn't—blame her for needing that.

The next morning, Crystal left to take the kids to school. No one was in the house. I went back into our bedroom, opened the closet door, and cleared away all the shoes on the floor. I shut the door behind me and got down on my knees in the darkness. Without hesitation, I opened up my heart and was more honest than I had ever been in my entire life. Truth overcame the lies as I cried out, "God, I can't . . . I can't do this. I can't do this alone. I can't do this without You. I need Your help. Please . . . please help me."

Growing up, I heard Dad tell stories about grown men, tough men, strong men coming to Jesus, about how they dropped to their hands and knees in brokenness and repentance. For many years I had been hung up on being cool and macho in the constant desire to act like a rock star. I never allowed myself to be in submission to anything. When I reflect on that moment of being on my face before the Lord, I know that was the manliest thing I have ever done. To submit. To humble myself. To give up my life.

I had no fancy or flowery words. I had nothing left to give except an empty heart—the only thing remaining of a broken and desperate man. For me, repeating a prayer after a pastor Sunday after Sunday never had the same effect as falling on my knees alone in that closet and crying out to God. Before, I always thought I must be doing something wrong, but I knew in that moment, this was finally *right*. I knew that I knew I was saved.

Jesus rescued me.

Growing up in church, I can't even tell you how many times I had said "the sinner's prayer." I walked down the aisle to the front on many Sundays, but my heart had never actually changed. Before, I had just gone along with what my friends were doing. I had done what I thought my parents and everyone at the church expected me to do. But this time I wasn't in front of a congregation but on my face at the feet of a King. I wasn't trying to please anyone except the One who had redeemed me, just like the song said. I cried out and reached up to the Father. *My* Father. *My* Savior. He was as real and as close to me as the breath in my lungs.

In my prayer of desperation in that hotel room in Europe, I had asked God to show me He was real, to prove He is who He says He is. He had done exactly that. In the moments after asking Jesus to come in and change me, I thought, "I don't have to go back and be that guy anymore. That Zach died today in the darkness of this closet. I'm walking out into the light as a new man."

So now, with the grace and mercy of Jesus, I knew I had to do what I'd promised—press on and never look back.

My old self has been crucified with Christ. It is no longer I who live, but Christ lives in me. So I live in this earthly body by trusting in the Son of God, who loved me and gave himself for me.

—GALATIANS 2:20

CHAPTER 8

LETTING GO AND DIGGING IN

But You walked right through the fire

Never thought of backing down

Yeah, You kept on coming for me

'Cause You knew love is a battleground[11]

With my substance abuse being at an eleven and now dropping to zero, the benefits of starting the right things and stopping the wrong things was working its way through many areas of my life. When I told Crystal I was done with the band, I meant what I said. I shut that door. In my new relationship with Jesus, in His grace and strength, I found a sense of confidence and security I had never experienced before. I had known what it was like to be good at basketball, believing I could go on the court, game after game, and win. I had experienced the same dynamic when I would walk out in front of a club full of people, grab my guitar, take the mic, and sell a song. But life was so different now. My sense of identity was coming from another Source. I not only had a strong motivation to change, but I *was* changing. For me, it was proof that God can take our stubborn flesh and give us His steadfast Spirit. We just have to surrender everything to Him.

A couple of days after my reckoning with God in the closet, I asked to have a band meeting. I got right to the point and told the guys the time had come for me to leave. They didn't see it coming and were caught off-guard, especially with me saying there was *no* discussion about continuing. Needless to say, the conversation did not go well. It hit the proverbial fan. Things went south quick and got ugly fast. When the meeting was over, I think the guys assumed that my decision wouldn't last, that this would eventually become an inside joke because I would come back in a week or so. But days turned into weeks, and soon they realized I wasn't bluffing. This was for real. It was over. Done. We canceled every booking, except for one final show that we played about a week later. After that night, Zach Williams and the Reformation parted ways.

When a band has been together for several years, along with being on the road that many days a year, and one person decides to call it quits, it's like a nasty divorce with five people involved. Besides the emotional aspect, there are assets to split up. For quite a while, I questioned myself, not in the decision but in how I handled it at the time. I wondered, "Could I have done it differently? Better? Or was a swift, clean break the only way?"

For me, the decision came down to the band or my family, and, clearly, I was choosing my family. The guys had won plenty of times, but not this time. I had to prove to Crystal and the kids that I loved them more than I loved the band or even my music. I wasn't about to lose them. I had to prove to everyone that I was willing to walk away from it all. And I knew God was telling me to close this chapter on my old life.

The truth is, with a few of the guys, we didn't have any communication for several years. But I am glad to report that we are now good with one another, with things understood and relationships repaired. We are each in a very different place in life than back then. I had dinner with all the guys over Christmas break in 2021. It was the first time we had all been in the same room since 2012. Some family members and friends had passed away, so the reality that life is short and old friendships are important brought us together. We all made amends. We eventually realized we were just being stubborn by holding on to our pride.

Bottom line is, there is no easy way to break up a band. But they finally understood that after we got back from Europe, I was in a place where I couldn't have survived if we had kept going. And they all now seem to respect the direction I took.

Years after the breakup, Red, whose conversation with me had started the ball rolling the night we met at the local bar, told me, "You were the first person we'd ever met who could silence a room when you started singing. We all saw something in you that first night. That's the reason why we changed the band. We knew something was going to happen with you. That's why it hurt so bad when you suddenly quit after we got back from Europe." Of course, I told him I understood how hard the situation was on all of us.

FACING THE MUSIC

The Bible sets a clear precedent for repentance—making an about-face in life to surrender everything to God, walking away from certain relationships, places, and circumstances to do what He is calling you to do. Ephesians 6:12 is clear that we never wrestle with flesh and blood, but only against evil itself. None of the guys in the band were ever enemies to me, or me to them. I made my own bad choices. While we all influenced one another, no one forced me to drink whiskey, smoke dope, take any substance, or do stupid things. That's on me.

To make the one-eighty that I knew my family and I desperately needed, and to truly pursue a relationship with Christ, I had no choice but to walk away from anyone or anything that might take me down that bad road again. The old saying "Burn the ships," meaning to destroy any path leading back to where you came from, makes a lot of sense. Whenever any of us make the tough decision to exit a situation for our own good, there will be some folks who won't or can't understand. But I've learned over the years that when God tells you it's time to end something, you need to be done. The same is true when He tells you to start something. You have to obey and then trust Him to sort everything out in His timing.

When the band ended, the only relationship that continued was with Robby, the one whose lead I had followed into this new life. He and his wife and Crystal and I kept going to church together. After that final show with the band, I didn't play music at all for the next six months. Honestly, it wasn't that hard to put down. I wanted nothing to do with it. I didn't pick up my guitar and I didn't sing anywhere. I closed the chapter. If God ever wanted me to play music again, He could turn the page and start it back up in His time. But that would be His call, not mine. Meanwhile, I went back to work for Dad full-time. Now even that was very different because I was clean and sober, following Jesus.

My new focus was my family, which in September 2012 became the six of us, with our daughter Delilah being born.

But first and foremost was my relationship with God. I knew if I worked every day to be obedient and put Him first, then everything else in life would fall into place. Matthew 6:33 can be one of those poster verses that we rattle off and don't really think about, but the truth in Jesus's statement is powerful.

Seek first his kingdom and his righteousness, and all these things will be given to you as well. (NIV)

For me, "all these things" were everything else in life after my relationship with the One I had to seek first. He's the Giver who will give us what we need, when we need it.

When I met Crystal, she struggled with the same things I did, so we understood each other. I think hanging in there together through so much bad stuff eventually proved our love for one another. So by the time we met the Lord, we both thought, "Oh, this is going to be a cakewalk. If we made it through all those years, then surely things can only get better from here."

When I began to follow Christ, for the first time in our relationship, I started really listening to Crystal and *hearing* her. I worked to understand what she had gone through and tried to put myself in her shoes. I gained a real respect for what she had to fight her way through to be the person she is and the fact that she's even still alive. I developed a compassion for her that I'd never experienced before. Through this new perspective, I gained an authentic appreciation for Crystal as a woman. A lot of what I hadn't understood before became clear. I hadn't realized she was doing the very best she knew how to survive because that was the way she was raised. She had kids to put first, so she wasn't thinking about anybody else. I didn't really grasp any of that until I saw her through the eyes of Jesus. But, once I did, I started to understand who Crystal is and what God had brought her through. I experienced a whole new love for my wife after our relationship was made new. All the toxic mess from all those years became out of sight, out of mind.

To this day, while we have walked through an incredible amount of healing, we keep working to make our marriage the best it can be. While we know our total transformation into the image of Christ won't happen until the day we die, meanwhile, I'm constantly working on *my* stuff, through the bad and the good that life brings.

From Crystal

When Zach had called to tell me about his transformation, I told him I had heard those kinds of promises before. I didn't believe him at first. But true to his commitment, when Zach got home, he quit the band, did the farewell show, and then put the old life behind him. He was literally transformed. Once Zach turned around and we plugged into the church, it was almost like God was accelerating life to make up for lost time.

After our encounter with the Lord, it was like
our spiritual eyes, our kingdom eyes, were opened.
From there, as Zach and I got on the same page, we
began a spiritual dance together. We've always been
in sync when we weren't butting heads, but this was
an entirely different level. God began to show us how
He had made us one. We each shared what we were
hearing from Him. If one of us felt led to do something
and talked to the other about it, often we would realize
we were thinking the same thing. Then we just talked
about *how*, not *what*. We quickly developed a spiritual
synergy together.

FINDING MY OWN FAITH

As Crystal and I committed to go to church every week with
Robby and his wife, we all decided to attend their five o'clock
service on Sunday afternoons. They called it the Loft because
it was in an intimate, upstairs area where the youth met. The
room had an urban vibe with a bunch of string lights dangling
from the ceiling. Starting out in that kind of environment,
with a smaller service, eased us into church. To move forward
in a real commitment to a local body of believers, I had to work
hard to overcome my long-term battle with religion. In our
transition to this new life, starting over in many ways, I had to
do a lot of personal soul-searching and healing.

I remember a time at church camp when I was around nine

or ten years old. During an evening service, at the invitation, I walked down to the front. Camp is good at creating moments for kids and teens where you feel all kinds of emotions. When you see your friends crying on their knees at the altar, it's easy to think, "I gotta do that. I need to go down there too." Any decision I had made growing up was due to the emotion of the moment. The power of peer pressure made me feel it was something I had to do. I didn't want to be the only kid who didn't "get saved" at church camp. But I didn't really know what I was doing. I didn't understand the commitment. Even though it was a positive step, I was just following the crowd.

As I got older, church had a weird dynamic for me. With my parents usually being friends with the pastors, I saw too much of the inside, the bad side. I heard one too many stories. But I also had trouble understanding why suddenly one Sunday we were going to a different church and would never go back to our old one. My parents changed churches several times over the years after various fallouts, over things that I began to feel were just religious differences.

When I moved out of my parents' house, I was suddenly free to make my own decisions. Like many young people, because I always felt forced to go to church, when I no longer had to attend, I opted out. During my years of rebellion when I would finally give in to my parents' invitation to meet them at church, as the sermon would start, I would always think, "How did he know I was going to be here today? Did my parents tell him? It's like he's preaching to me." I didn't like that feeling of being paranoid and thinking that everyone was staring at me. However it happened, hearing a message that was too on the nose and too intense was scary. So I rarely went because I didn't want to deal with those feelings.

Yet throughout my twenties into my early thirties, no matter what shape my life was in at the time, no matter how bad or good things were, if anyone asked me about my faith or where I stood with Jesus, my stock answer was always that I "had my own personal relationship with Him." From growing up in a Christian home and my parents being on the worship team, I knew enough of the buzz words people were looking for to satisfy most of them. And being on the road almost every weekend for so many years was a good excuse for why I was never in church.

When I was in the band, my hair was long and wild. With that, and the way I dressed, I know I looked rough. One time, after my parents had left the church where I grew up because of some fallout or scandal, they invited me to visit their new one. I agreed to go with them. After the service they introduced me to the pastor, and as I shook his hand, he looked me up and down. I could literally feel his judgment. I remember thinking, "I'm not going to go somewhere that I don't feel like I'm good enough." That moment stuck in my head and would replay anytime the subject of church came up.

Then there was the added issue of people talking behind my parents' backs about me, saying things like, "Why does the worship leader have a son who lives like that, who looks like that?" I know it was hard for my dad and mom to see some of those things the way I did. They just wanted me to be in church with them and for me to get my life right with the Lord because they loved me. They would often tell me I had just misunderstood or misread the pastor or some of the members. But I felt differently.

I always saw that because my dad could lead worship, he had value to the church they attended. But to me, it felt like if you weren't some kind of resource to the pastor or the congregation, then you weren't good enough to be there. The very people who most need the message of the church cannot be the same people judged and rejected when they walk in. I often wondered if that's what Jesus thought about the Pharisees when they treated those He came to save in that same way.

During those final difficult days in Europe, as I wrestled with God and tried to assess my faith, I had to face the reality that I had *no* relationship with Christ. I had to be honest and confess there was no fruit to show for my life. In fact, everything pointed to the opposite. If I had ever been accused of being a Christian, there wouldn't have been enough evidence to convict me. I spent no time reading the Word, praying, or pursuing any kind of spiritual growth. I knew what pastors and the Christians around me said I needed to believe, but I never received it for myself. My parents lived out their faith, but I had none of my own. Like the old preacher's saying goes, "God ain't got no grandchildren." I never dug in and discovered what Jesus meant to me. Like anything that's important in life, you have to come to your own conclusion as to what you believe, because God loves us enough and gives each of us the freedom to choose Him or reject Him.

Because of all this bad history and emotional baggage, I had to overcome my associating church with legalism, not grace; with religion, not a relationship. I had to get past the times growing up when I felt like I had to go down front every Sunday to get right with God—again—but simply didn't understand the reality of a personal, onetime commitment to Jesus and living the life of being His disciple between salvation and heaven. I had to relearn what the body of Christ was meant to be and how I had a home there. I had to realize that the biggest place of rejection in my past could become my safest place of acceptance in the present.

When I was young, I didn't yet understand what I needed to be saved *from*. I hadn't lived enough life to grasp what the cross meant or what Jesus had done for me. But after deciding to drop out of high school and walking through hell on earth for a decade, I came to a real understanding of why I needed salvation, why I needed rescue. I had to come to the end of myself and realize that no matter how hard I try to get right with God, I can't do it by myself. I can't work hard enough to earn His love, because He's never going to love me more than He already does. The cross cost Jesus everything so grace could be given to me for free.

For a long time, looking at life only through the rearview mirror was hard. The what-ifs were a killer. What if I had finished high school? What if I had gotten a basketball scholarship from a major university? What if I had been a college basketball star? Could I have made it to the NBA? What if I had gotten a sports degree and become a coach? The what-ifs can keep you up at night, second-guessing your life.

But then here's the other side of the what-ifs that prove God's protection: What if I had overdosed? What if I'd been killed in a bar? What if I'd been arrested? What if I had become an alcoholic or addict? What if I hadn't met Crystal? What if I hadn't gone to Europe that last time? What if I hadn't prayed that day? What if I hadn't come to the end of myself and looked up?

That's why I will never forget June 10, 2012, as the day I knew for sure I had received the truth of the gospel. I feel like my life began when I said yes to Jesus at thirty-three years old.

With God, Nothing Is Wasted

As Crystal and I became more and more involved in the life of the church, before long, if the doors were open, we were there. As the church leadership found out more about us, they asked us to share our testimonies, individually and together. The goal was to reach those who felt like their lives were hopeless and beyond God's help. Crystal and I knew if God could transform us, He could do the same for anyone. We became the old analogy of beggars who had found the banquet and just wanted everyone to know where the food is. We couldn't keep Jesus a secret. We had to share Him.

I think some people at the church almost couldn't believe how much we had changed. Of course, we were still raw and rough around the edges, but our hearts totally belonged to Jesus now. When we shared our testimonies, Crystal and I would talk about things you aren't supposed to talk about in church. But, to us, those were the very things people need to hear to know how much God loves us and wants to rescue us. (And, of course, sharing that message is our only goal with this book too.) For the past several decades, many churches have worked to act like the dirty side of sin doesn't exist, and that approach has never and will never work to reach unbelievers. That has caused many people in desperate need of help to feel like they aren't good enough to walk into a gathering of God's people. So I think Crystal and I sharing the good, the bad, and the ugly so openly was refreshing to a lot of people.

After we were at the church for several months, the pastor asked me to sing a song. I felt like I was ready and agreed. No surprise that I decided the best choice for my first time on a church stage was to sing "Redeemed," the song God had used to get my attention and draw me to His love. I figured if the song had spoken to me, it could speak to others like me that had come that Sunday.

The next time the pastor asked me to sing, he requested a specific song to go with the service that day. He asked me to learn "Lifesong" by the Christian band Casting Crowns. But he didn't tell me anything else about the service, and I had no idea what I was getting myself into. That Sunday, when I went out and sang the song with the worship band, people started walking up on the stage, one by one, participating in what is known as "cardboard testimonies," where each participant writes a short statement of faith and holds it up in front of them.

Folks held up signs that told everyone how God had helped them get sober, saved their marriage, and other specific ways

He had radically changed their lives—each with a short, simple message. Watching the people walk up and show their signs as I sang, I became emotional. It was tough to make it through the song. I'm not sure it would have been any easier had I known ahead of time, because I could relate to each of the people and how God had done something powerful in their lives to change them.

The whole experience was so moving. I remember thinking afterward, "That was the same feeling I had as a kid, the way a church service would move me and make me feel." But this time I was okay. Maybe that was what God was trying to tell me all those years ago that I never understood? That I needed to be drawn to those feelings in my heart instead of feeling like I had to run away from them.

As I grew in my faith, a lot of events from my past started making sense. I was able to look back and see all these little moments where I didn't realize God was working at the time. That's when I began to see that nothing I had gone through had been wasted. There was a reason behind everything, the successes *and* the failures. There was a reason I didn't "make it" in my old band, because money and fame would have led me straight into self-destruction. The more spiritual maturity I gained, the more I was able to see how God had been present and active throughout my life. The dots were connecting, giving all the craziness a purpose.

I also wondered if maybe there was something more to what I felt that Sunday morning singing "Lifesong" and how people responded.

God saved you by his grace when you believed. And you can't take credit for this; it is a gift from God. Salvation is not a reward for the good things we have done, so none of us can boast about it. For we are God's masterpiece. He has created us anew in Christ Jesus, so we can do the good things he planned for us long ago.

—Ephesians 2:8–10

CHAPTER 9

WHEN GOD WRITES YOUR STORY

If you've been walking the same old road for miles and miles
If you've been hearing the same old voice tell the same old lies
If you're trying to fill the same old holes inside
There's a better life[12]

By the spring of 2013, starting the second year in our new life with Christ, I had sung only two times at our church on a Sunday morning with the worship team. But God had begun to stir my heart to write new songs. Through music, I wanted to talk about my experience and what I was discovering about a relationship with Jesus. When I had a few songs finished, I went to a studio and recorded an EP. I called the project *Zach Williams and the Brothers of Grace, working with Robby and other musicians from the church*. I wanted to put out some songs centered on my faith to see what would happen. One of them was called "Washed Clean."

During this season, Crystal had signed up at church to go with a small team on a Sunday afternoon to give her testimony at a women's prison. As she told me her plans, she ended with, "And you should go with me." At the time, while I didn't yet know anything specific God wanted me to do other than continue being obedient, I didn't think prison ministry was for me. So I answered her, half joking, "I worked so hard for years to stay out of prison! Why would I want to voluntarily go in now?" We laughed and the discussion was over.

When that Sunday afternoon rolled around, Crystal went and I stayed home with the kids. When she came home, she was excited. She couldn't stop talking about what she had experienced at the prison. Her heart was on fire for the women she had met. As she finished telling me the stories, Crystal said, "Zach, next time, I'm signing you and I up to go together. You can play some of your new songs, and we can share our story."

When the next opportunity was announced, just as she said she would, Crystal put both our names on the list. The church's connections pastor had become a good friend of ours and worked hard to invest in me and Crystal to help us heal and grow. He was with us that day, along with Robby, who came to play guitar with me. Because Robby had worked on the *Brothers of Grace* EP with me, he already knew the songs.

In front of a room full of incarcerated women, Crystal and I shared our story of what God had done, and was doing, in our lives. When we finished, we gave an invitation to come to Christ as Robby and I played "Washed Clean." As I often do, I closed my eyes while I was singing. At some point later in the song, I looked out to see around thirty women down on their knees at the altar, giving their lives to the Lord. God had clearly shown up in that room in a powerful way. I was so amazed and moved by what was happening, I could barely finish the song. To this day, that's a part of the life with Christ that *never* gets old. Every time feels like the first time when you witness Him at work, touching people's hearts. Which is exactly the opposite experience of all those years I was chasing after that elusive "first-time high" feeling.

That moment when I opened my eyes, I felt like God showed me my purpose and my future. Like Crystal said before, I had an aha moment. I believe He told me, "Zach, *this* is it. These are the songs, the places, the stories, the people I want you to reach." The message was unmistakable: He was telling me what He wanted me to do with my music, with my life. That day was also the beginning of Crystal and I sharing a heart for prison ministry together.

Around that same time, the church hosted a Celebrate Recovery group that met in a house on the church's property. We started sharing at those meetings, and I would sing my new songs. At these gatherings, I also led worship, which was new for me.

Reaching out to the broken and hurting folks in our community had developed into a theme of our lives. When people would ask Crystal and me why we thought God was showing up at these places where we were ministering, my answer always had to do with the transparency that we chose to offer. Being open about past mistakes, we realized, all too often, is something people in the church are just not willing to do. A lot of folks were a little taken aback by how raw and real we were in that first year or two. We didn't have any area of life where we would say, "Whoa! We don't talk about *that* here." We just wanted to share the truth with people about what God could do in their lives. For us to act like we never had any problems or didn't go through something hard would not be authentic. We were willing to be open about our past for the sake of the gospel. And that was something a lot of people seemed to latch onto. I can't tell you how many times we had people come up to us and say, "Wow, this is what church is *supposed* to be."

Something inside me needed to confess and get rid of all the pain and baggage I had stored up from the many years of running from God. Being a part of all these ministries had a healing effect on me, giving me a chance to talk about the tough issues and get them out in the open. There was *nothing* I was trying to hide anymore. When I came to Jesus, I wanted to be done lying about my life. As I say in the song "Washed Clean," God offers a constant cleansing for the soul.

When I started being honest about where I had come from and what I had walked through, I realized how many other people in the church needed to do the same thing. While I was helping myself, I was helping others too, leading by example. I wasn't really trying to do that, it just happened. When we follow Christ, we don't become perfect, and we never will until heaven. But the masks people wore was what kept me away from church for so many years, so now I was trying to be real to draw in folks like me. With my new freedom in Christ, I felt like I had nothing to lose and everything to gain, as Paul tells us in Philippians 3:8.

DIDN'T SEE *THAT* COMING

One Sunday after church, the pastor found me and said, "Zach, we've been watching you and Crystal for a while now as you've been involved with the prison ministry and Celebrate Recovery. We've seen how much your family has grown and matured. We all feel like God has placed you here. We've been wanting to launch a new campus for a long time, but we've not been able to find the right fit for some of the leadership positions. We feel like with your story, you two can reach people we can't. Zach, would you help us launch this campus by being involved with the worship and the music? Would you come on staff with us here part-time at the church?"

I had a *lot* of questions, especially about our past and how that would affect our involvement with the church staff. Plus, at that point, I didn't consider myself a "worship leader," either as a role or as a job title. To all my rapid-fire questions, the pastor just kept saying, "Don't worry, Zach, we'll figure that out." Finally, he offered, "Starting out, we won't call you a pastor, we'll call you a director. There's a full-time pastor you'd be working with." The plan was to keep my job with Dad but also to have specific music responsibilities with this new service. Fast-forward—the church staff made it happen, and I helped them launch a new service called the Refuge.

The service met on the church campus in the basketball gym. Because of the people we were trying to reach, everything we did was a totally different style than what was happening in the main sanctuary. As soon as we launched the service, people began to show up. We were definitely hitting the target, as most of them were "outsiders" for various reasons: people who had never been able to find their place in a church, people who had never been involved in anything connected to a church. Folks from Celebrate Recovery came, and also some of the inmates we had ministered to came after getting out of prison. To no surprise, considering my testimony, we also attracted a lot of musicians and bikers. The

Refuge reminded me of Jesus's parable in Matthew 22 where the king tells his servants to go out and invite the people off the street to come to his banquet—the good and the bad alike. Just open up the doors, because everyone is welcome here. I wanted to provide a place that the old Zach Williams would have been able to walk in and be welcomed, not judged.

In that season of ministry, I learned one major lesson about God and how He seems to work, something I didn't understand for so long. The biggest reason or excuse that keeps too many of us from saying yes to what God calls us to do is that we don't feel "qualified" or "prepared." We worry that we won't have the right words to say or know what to do. We focus on what *we can't* do instead of what *He can* do. Many of us try to ignore God's voice when He just wants to hear us say, "Yes, Lord, I'll do it," and to simply trust Him for whatever is next, getting ready to go do whatever He says.

I learned through prison ministry and Celebrate Recovery that when I say yes to God, I may not have any idea what I'm going to do or say. But after the yes, He always works everything out and gives me the words. When the pastor came to us that day with his invitation, my first response was, "But I'm not qualified to do any of this. I don't belong in leadership. This is not something I feel comfortable doing." Yet when I stopped asking all the questions and just said yes, God Himself qualified me and gave me everything I needed. And He's still doing that.

Because of the yes, the first time I led worship onstage was the first time I felt completely comfortable in my own skin playing music. After a decade of playing to thousands of people in the US and Europe in bars and clubs, to emphasize, that moment with God was the first time I felt *completely* comfortable playing music. That was because it was the first time I had truly submitted to the reason He created me. I realized that when I lead worship, the music isn't about *me*. There is a vertical relationship happening.

Bottom line—God just wants to hear each of us say yes. And I'm here to tell you, there's nothing else like it when we do.

With the focus on reaching people who were living just like Crystal and I had for many years, the growth of the Refuge exploded. It wasn't long before we maxed out the room and had to add a second service. After the first year, the church decided to move the other pastor to another campus. They asked me to come on staff full-time, becoming my first "real job," one with a salary and benefits. I thought, "Man, this is all I could ever dream of. Serving the Lord and playing music with a regular paycheck twice a month. This is the best thing in the world."

Because the money I made working for Dad was more than the new salary, I had to take a pay cut to be full-time with the church. The one positive was that they offered good insurance benefits. To make up for the shortfall, Crystal decided to get her real estate license. That career would also allow her the flexibility to work around the kids' schedules.

On Sundays at the Refuge, after I led worship with the band, the pastor's message from the main campus was broadcast on a large screen in the gym. Guys from local bands began coming to the church, as well as people who knew us from our past life. Because Crystal and I were the leaders, they felt safe. We weren't playing "church shuffle" by just attracting people from other congregations, but rather reaching the "unchurched" unbelievers. Eventually, I was able to form a worship band from local players who started bringing their families.

Along with the two Refuge services on Sunday, I also started leading worship every week for the college Bible study, as well as ministering to the people from our service throughout the week, along with performing some office duties. From time to time, I helped out in the main service in front of their huge crowds. The biggest audience the band had ever played for didn't compare to the several thousand people in those church services.

God was clearly at work, and we were just trying to keep up.

From Crystal

What drew the church leadership to Zach was that he was so different, outside their box. But fitting in with the other staff members was hard for him. Being from a blue-collar world, he wanted to just walk into a pastor's office, sit down, and talk face-to-face, but they wanted him to send an email and wait for the response. The very reason they hired him for the

Refuge was also what caused him not to fit in with the staff. He struggled with some depression while he was doing his best to adjust to a totally different environment.

But God certainly put us on the fast track. He knew where we were going. It was miraculous. All these crazy things began to happen because He had taken over. Yet the way God opened doors for us and the way He worked through us to reach others weren't the only miracles we saw in that season. As Zach mentioned, he took a pay cut to work for the church. With raising four kids, we sometimes had only fifty dollars to get through two weeks. But God would always come through. One time I found $1,500 in an old coat of mine, which made me wonder, "When did I ever have that much cash to just stash in my pocket?" Those circumstances taught me not to be afraid because He was going to be sure we were fine.

WHEN GOD SHOWS UP

On December 24, 2014, another event happened that we never would have imagined in our wildest dreams.

A few weeks prior, the pastor and the worship pastor at the church had asked me to be a part of leading the Christmas Eve services, which would be held in the main auditorium that afternoon and evening. They asked me to sing. This was the first time I was given such a visible role at the main campus. I chose the song and put together a custom arrangement with the worship band.

Jonathan Smith, a Christian music producer and songwriter in Nashville who grew up in Jonesboro, had come home for Christmas to visit family. Because his father-in-law was a deacon at the church, they attended one of the services that night. Their family had planned on going to a different campus but at the last minute chose to attend the main service. For some reason, they decided to drive across town to attend where I would be singing.

During the service, Jonathan and his wife noticed me. One of the reasons is that I was much taller than everyone else. His wife nudged him and asked, "Who's the big dude?" "I don't know. Don't recognize him," he answered. When it came time for my song in the service, I stepped up to the mic and poured out my heart. Evidently, with their initial intrigue about me and then after hearing me sing, Jonathan wanted to know more.

Right after Christmas, he called the church and asked for my email address. He sent me a message about hearing my song at the service, then added, "I'm from Jonesboro too, but now I live in Nashville. I write and produce Christian music. I'd love to visit with you while I'm here this week."

By that point, I had been hit up by quite a few people making promises about a music career, but nothing ever panned out. Although I was new to Christian music, I was a veteran in the music business after spending many years as a touring and recording artist. After I read Jonathan's email, I thought, "I've heard this a hundred times from people, but what the heck? I'll meet with him." So, a couple of days after Christmas, before he and his family went back to Nashville, Jonathan and I met at a coffee shop.

I shared my entire crazy story with him. Afterward, he said, "Man, you should come to Nashville so we can write together." Unfortunately, my old life was coming back to bite me by getting in the way of this new opportunity. From all the years of doing drywall, I had blown out a disc in my neck. I already had surgery scheduled, and the recovery would take a while. I told Jonathan I was all in but would have to wait until I was healed up enough to drive.

It was hard to put this offer aside for now. As I've said, more than singing or performing, songwriting has always been my passion. I love coming up with an idea and then crafting a song line by line, chord by chord, to share some part of the gospel in a unique way. There's a beautiful connection to the Creator when we start with a blank page and a headful of chords, then end up telling a story in four minutes that has the potential of impacting countless lives over many years. That's exactly why music is a powerful and passionate tool to reach the world. And it all starts with a song.

As I was quickly learning, God's timing is always perfect. Jonathan told me his wife was pregnant and he also had to wait to get together. For the next six months, we kept in touch, getting past my recovery and the arrival of their new baby. Finally, in the summer of 2015, I started going to Nashville for us to write songs together. By my third trip, Jonathan had reached out to his songwriting buddies and invited some of them to join us for cowriting sessions. For an entire week, we worked every day with someone different.

On my last day before going back to Arkansas, Jonathan had invited Mia Fieldes, a respected and popular songwriter who had moved to Nashville from her home in Australia. During the week, several of the other writers had brought up Mia, and everyone talked about how talented she was. Because of her reputation, I was a little nervous going into the writing session. Full transparency: by that final writing session, I had used up all the ideas I had brought with me. So for the first hour or so, I just shared my story with Mia as Jonathan listened in. When I was done, she talked about her connection to people who had dealt with substance abuse and how hopeless life can become.

Out of the blue, Mia said, "You should write a song called 'Chain Breaker.'" While I stopped to let the idea sink in, she continued, "As big as you are, everybody's going to believe you! . . . And with your story, that name for God with what He's done in your life just makes sense."

Agreeing with her, I asked, "Well, okay, so how does it go?" Immediately, Jonathan started playing the chords that became the intro to the song. When I heard the melody, I sang, "If you've been walkin' the same old road for miles and miles," the words that became the first line. We all stopped and looked at each other with a "What just happened?" look on our faces. From there, it was like God just took over and wrote the song for us. Literally in about fifteen minutes, "Chain Breaker" was finished, as if He were downloading the lyrics and melody and we were just trying to catch it.

Because we were writing at Jonathan's studio, we recorded a demo of me singing the song. The next day as I drove home, I prayed all the way back for God to show me what He was doing with all this. Something was up. Something was going on. I could feel it.

After I had made several trips to meet Jonathan at the Provident office in Franklin, a suburb of Nashville, eventually some of the staff asked him, "Hey, who's the big dude you've been bringing in here?" Jonathan told them I was a new songwriter buddy he was working with. Blaine Barcus, an artist representative at Provident, had become curious about me after Jonathan played him a few of our demos. Blaine asked me if he could come to Arkansas and visit the worship service I led. He wanted to talk and explore the potential of me becoming a Christian artist. Of course, I agreed, because in all my trips there and all the people I had met, no one else had shown an interest in me.

We had written "Chain Breaker" in early September 2015. In November, Blaine came to visit me at the church and spent some time schooling me on how the Christian music industry typically worked. He explained about putting a band together, coming up with the strongest set of original songs, and then scheduling a showcase to invite labels to come hear me. But he also painted a realistic yet bleak picture of how few artists are actually signed and then, even if they are, how it can take years to see anything happen. No promises and no guarantees. Because of his long career in the business, he informed me that if I was going to go down the artist road, I needed to settle in for the long haul and be prepared to make some major sacrifices. The good news was I figured he must be telling me all this because he felt like I had a shot at making it.

A couple of days after he went back to Nashville, I was at church on a Wednesday night getting ready to lead worship for a college service when my phone rang. It was Blaine. He said, "Zach, you aren't going to believe this—and like I told you, this hardly ever happens—but we had a label meeting yesterday. We played some of your songs and the demo of 'Chain Breaker.' Terry Hemmings, the head of the label, called our attorney and told him to draft a record contract for you. He said, 'It's a matter of time before someone else hears this guy and signs him, so we need to jump on it.'"

Blaine ended with, "Brother, you're being offered a record deal from Provident. Welcome to the family!"

From Crystal

Not long before that Christmas when Jonathan and his family came to the service, Zach had come to the place of saying he didn't need to pursue a record deal or music career. So it was almost as if God said, "Oh, I'm glad you feel that way. Now I can let you have the desires of your heart." When Zach gave in and surrendered every aspect of his talent, that's when God gave him the record deal.

When Zach came home from writing "Chain Breaker," he told me he knew something special was going on. He'd had the same feeling about the song that we had on that day when he sang "Washed Clean" at the prison and all those women had given their lives to Christ. God was in it.

One day while writing together in Nashville, Jonathan asked Zach, "I can tell songwriting is your biggest focus, but would you ever consider being an artist? Because these songs you're writing aren't going to fit very many Christian artists, but they do fit you." Zach was honest with him: "I don't know if I really want to do that anymore."

Right after that, Zach got a call from a friend he had toured with who was now working for a country record label. He wanted to talk about Zach possibly becoming the lead singer of a new band that a major country producer was going to work with. While that was a huge invitation and very encouraging, it was also a major test. Zach and I talked and agreed that we didn't need the distraction and should stay the course. But the timing was interesting. Not long after that is when Zach met with Blaine Barcus, and, as they say, the rest is history.

The kids and I were also at church when Blaine called Zach with the news. I immediately told our son,

"Now, don't say anything until Daddy has a chance to talk to the staff, okay?" He turned and ran out into the hallway, telling everyone, "My daddy just got a record deal!" So everyone at the church found out that night. Out of the mouths of babes.

BUCKLE UP AND HANG ON

In February 2016, I signed my Christian music recording contract. Terry Hemmings told Jonathan and me that they wanted to release "Chain Breaker" as my first single. He wanted that song, along with a full album, recorded as soon as possible. So we scheduled session players and went to Blackbird Studio, a popular recording facility in Nashville. But after everyone involved in the project heard the newest version, we all felt like the original demo still had the best performance of the song. I ended up recording a new lead vocal three different times in three studios, but we made the call to go back to the original vocal I had done at Jonathan's on the day we wrote the song. Everything we had added took away from that first recording. So we went back to the passion and purity that God had allowed us to capture organically on that first day.

Having no idea if this new adventure in Christian music would be successful, Crystal and I made the decision, for the security of our family, that I would stay on staff at the church for the time being. We trusted that God was at work in all this, but we also didn't want to be presumptuous of Him either. I talked with the leadership of the church, and we decided that I would go back to part-time for the Refuge, allowing me time to play shows. I also agreed to make every effort to be back on Sunday mornings to lead worship. I remember early on, while attending a Christian radio conference in Orlando, sitting down with my booking agents at a breakfast meeting. I told them all, "Look, I just want to be able to play music, make a living, and provide for my family."

For quite a while, we had been putting Crystal's real estate commissions into our savings account. With a move being likely, we had decided we should take some of the money and fix up our house to get it in shape to sell. Once we had some repairs and updates done, we then took the rest of the money and paid off all our debt. The good news was we owed no money except for our mortgage. The bad news was we had very little money left. We also knew the equity from our home wasn't going to be significant, certainly not enough to help us live off that first year of me playing music.

The single of "Chain Breaker" went to Christian radio in June 2016. Once the song hit number one, it stayed there for fifteen weeks. My second single, "Old Church Choir," became the most successful Christian radio single in over a decade after being at number one for twenty weeks. That made the song the second-longest-running number one single in *Billboard*'s Christian radio history. Because of the success of those songs, I became the first debut artist to have two back-to-back number one singles. The concept videos for both songs were also released. The *Chain*

Breaker record won a Grammy Award for Best Contemporary Christian Album in 2018.[13]

With the crazy success of the two radio singles, offers to tour started pouring in. Because the band and crew we had put together were all based in Nashville, I had to go back and forth from Arkansas to meet them anytime we left for a show. Then, when we returned, I always had a five-hour drive home. If we were leaving again in a day or two, going back to Jonesboro often made no sense. That made the stretches away from my family even longer.

In early spring of 2017, when I was on Chris Tomlin's Worship Night in America tour, Crystal and I had a heart-to-heart. She finally said, "Zach, we need to move because you're never at home anymore. We've all had enough. We need to be where you can come straight from the bus to be home with your family." I listened and knew she was right. This would be a huge move for us all, but God was clearly leading us into this new chapter of me becoming a Christian artist as our calling.

Crystal listed our house and received a contract the next day. When she called to tell me the news, I said, "Okay, this is happening. We're going to have to do this now." When I got home from the tour, I would talk to the church staff and tell them our plans. I would be leaving a job with benefits, plus Crystal and I had agreed that when we moved to Nashville, she was going to homeschool the kids. Because she would not be able to continue to sell real estate, we had no guarantee that this move would work financially. It was a *huge* step of faith for us.

From Crystal

Now, at thirty-eight years old, after being in the music business for years, Zach didn't walk in the door in Nashville naive and green. He's smart. But God also placed the best people around us, and we're all close. Everyone cares about each other. God has kept us safe and taught us what we needed to know. I feel like He had prepared me for Zach to be a touring artist. I don't have any anxiety like I did when he was with the band. Everything is different. I don't worry about him being gone now. I tell him, "Go do what you gotta do." I was always supportive of his music. The problem was the way he was doing his music. Really, it wasn't the music at all, it was life. I have so much respect for Zach. He became a totally different person. We're both completely different people. When God said in 2 Corinthians 5:17 that we are made new in Christ, that's not just a metaphor.

There's a purpose behind the music now. I feel like it's our ministry. Many people feel like they have to keep doing, doing, doing for God when He just wants us to be there in the moment, being faithful to what He calls us to do in the season we're in. We have to just rest in Him. He doesn't expect us to save the world. That's what He does. Even if your whole life is spent helping one person and that is the only thing God wants you to do, it's okay.

When I sat down and shared our new plans with the church staff, they were supportive and offered a generous idea. They asked me to play a concert with the worship band to which they would sell tickets. The proceeds would go to our family as a going-away gift. The concert was a success, and they sent us off with enough money to pay for our insurance for an entire year. That was an incredible blessing, just one example of God's provision. The church staff also told me anytime my schedule allowed, I was welcome to come back and lead worship. I could be an artist-in-residence, playing anytime I could come back in town. I was able to take them up on that offer a few times.

In May 2017, we moved into a rental home outside of Franklin to give us time to figure out our new life and get the lay of the land in the middle Tennessee area. Our new life was beginning.

One thing was certain—I knew I had not done anything to make all this happen. I hadn't gone to Nashville uninvited, knocking on doors, schmoozing people, going all over town working the room. Everything that had occurred—from the pastors asking me to lead a service, to Jonathan showing up at the Christmas Eve service, to Blaine coming to visit me, to Jonathan inviting Mia to write with us, to her suggesting "Chain Breaker," to the Provident staff hearing the demo, and finally Terry deciding to offer me a deal—that was *all* God at work. While a lot of people were involved in His plan, no one can take credit for bringing all the pieces together. It was *all* Him. It was all *about* Him.

After coming home from Europe, leaving the band, focusing on my family, and setting music aside, I fully surrendered my future to God. In His ways and in His time, He gave music back to me. And this time I would use it to glorify Him. That's exactly what redemption can do.

Faith shows the reality of what we hope for; it is the evidence of things we cannot see.

—HEBREWS 11:1

CHAPTER 10

THERE WAS JESUS

————————

Every minute, every moment
Of where I've been and where I'm going
Even when I didn't know it or couldn't see it
There was Jesus[14]

————————

One common thread throughout the different seasons of my life was working for Dad. Once I committed to Christ and the health of my family, getting off the road and away from music, I went all in, working with Dad in a way I never had before. Since I had started working full-time as a teenager after leaving high school, for the first time ever at thirty-three years old, I focused on putting in a solid eight hours, working hard, clean, and sober. No more sneaking in smoke breaks every two hours to stay high. I was just grateful to be alive and productive. And there was certainly no more argument about what station was playing on our work radio. We played Contemporary Christian or gospel music, which had always been Dad's first choice. My commitment to Jesus had become evident to everyone around me. The change was real.

In the introduction of this book, I shared about my talk from the stage in Columbus, Georgia, which was about the most important conversation my dad and I ever had. Now that we're safely on the Jesus side of my life and I've shared the calling He has placed on me and my family, I want to revisit that moment, to share more about my dad, and to reveal that entire discussion and the impact it had on me.

One day on a job site, Dad and I stopped for lunch. We went outside to eat, sitting down on a stack of sheetrock.

He suddenly became serious and looked a bit emotional. Something was clearly weighing heavily on his mind. I could tell he was working to form whatever he needed to say, so finally, I asked, "Dad? . . . Is everything okay?" He said, "Son, there's something I need to tell you. I think it's time you knew."

Dad began, "When your mom and I lived in Pensacola and I was going to Bible college, the church we went to had a baby dedication Sunday. You weren't even a year old. So we decided that was the right thing for us to do—to commit your life and our lives as parents to the Lord. On the way to the front of the church to join the pastor and the others, you started getting fussy. Then you began to cry and make a lot of noise. Just before the pastor was about to start, with your mom and I doing our best to calm you down, you let out a yell, a scream. The pastor paused, smiled, and said, 'Sounds like Zach's got a strong set of lungs on him. Probably going to be a singer someday.' We laughed, along with the church. But then his countenance changed and he became serious, as if he were listening to something, or Someone.

"Zach, the pastor looked right at us and stated, 'This child will be a voice for his generation.'"

As Dad went silent to allow the story to sink in, I was stunned. I believe he also paused to take in the fact that he had finally said what he had been holding in for so long. I swallowed hard and with a deep sense of humility asked him, "Why are you just now telling me this?"

It's Not about Me, It's about Jesus

From this point in the story, I want to go past what I shared from stage. I want to take you through the entire conversation between Dad and me that day. In the introduction of the book, the reference of the prodigal son is from Jesus's parable in Luke 15. Maybe you're a prodigal son or daughter. Or a prodigal's father or mother. Or the older brother who feels like you've been overlooked in your obedience. Maybe you haven't said yes to Jesus, just like me in my first three decades. Regardless of how you might identify in your faith or lack of it, I believe there's something of value in this exchange between Dad and me for each of us.

Tears streamed down Dad's cheeks as he answered, "Zach, I know now that I don't have to worry anymore if something were to happen to you. I don't need to be concerned that I would never see you again. Now I *know* where you're going. The same place I'm going. I've been holding on to this story for thirty-three years because I didn't want to tell you when you were out playing bars. I never wanted to put any kind of spiritual pressure on you or hand you something that could make you feel like you would have to live up to a standard when you weren't there yet. I had to wait on God's timing over all these years, but lately I've felt like it was finally the right time. The pastor's words were the reason I always told you that the Lord has a big plan for your life. It's also why I always said, if He *did* tell you, you couldn't handle it. You had to come into your own relationship with Jesus, and now you have. Zach, God is faithful."

More amazed than ever at Dad's long-suffering and grace, I listened intently as he continued, "I never really knew *when* I was going to tell you, but now it's time for you to understand that there's a bigger picture to all these things going on in your life right now. Ever since you were born, God has had this plan for your life, son. From around the age of nineteen to now at thirty-three—fourteen very long and hard years—there were many days I was afraid of getting a call that you were dead. Anytime you didn't show up for work and I couldn't reach you, I worried that the day I dreaded had come.

"When you were in college and you came by the house to ask for my old guitar, God reminded me of the prophecy. And later, when I realized you were playing, singing, and even writing songs, I knew the word the pastor shared from God about you was taking root. I saw how He could fulfill His promise when you started playing music. I hadn't thought too much about it until then. That gift made sense, because music can be such a powerful medium that causes people all over the world to listen.

"When you were twenty years old and decided to stop playing basketball and start playing music, God used that circumstance to put the prophecy back on my heart for you. I remembered that moment holding you as a baby in front of everyone at the church. I remembered every word that had been spoken over your life. But then when you started writing blues and rock songs and living the way you were, I prayed,

'Lord, why is Zach using Your gift for *this*? I don't understand.'
But I knew I had to just watch and wait for the day I prayed
would come for you . . . And it has."

As Dad shared, I remembered the many times over the
years when my parents had come to a club where I was playing.
They would drink coffee to pay for their seats and listen to me
for hours, all while I was getting drunk up onstage, running up
a bar tab that was more than I would be paid for the night. But
no matter my behavior, they were supportive and proud of my
talent.

After holding in so many feelings and emotions for such a
long time, Dad kept pouring out his heart to me. "For all those
years, Zach, I knew there was something more coming for you.
Because you don't just pick up an instrument at that age and
start singing with the kind of voice that no one even knew you
had at the time. But every time I heard your strong, soulful,
passionate sound in those clubs, I would just go home and pray.
Every time, I asked God to show me what in the world was going
on with you. I wanted so badly to know when His promise was
going to be delivered. But often, trying to pin the blame on why
it wasn't happening, I would point the finger at myself. I would
ask, 'Lord, what did I do wrong as a father? I believe I've done
everything You've asked me to do. Yet here he is, living this life.
This can't be all there is for him. When, Lord?'"

Like a lot of fathers and sons, Dad and I certainly had our
differences over the years. But I always loved working with
him. We had a lot of good days together on his job sites. Dad
never judged me and was always available for a father-son life

lesson filled with grace. He never preached at me. Knowing how I was living, he just kept praying. Even though he easily could have, Dad never once made a threat like, "If you don't come to church with us, I'm going to fire you." He never used my job as leverage. Rather, it was always to my benefit, because no matter what I did, he kept me on to make sure I had a paycheck. Once again, constant grace.

There were days that I didn't belong on anyone's job site, and my choices would force Dad to send me home. He would see the shape I was in and say, "Son, you don't need to be here. Go home." I would get embarrassed or mad and storm off. But I always came back, and he would welcome me with open arms. I was the prodigal son who just *kept* leaving and then coming back home. Dad always responded by saying, "Zach, I don't have an answer for you other than Jesus." Now, in the end, he was right. Jesus *was* the only answer.

Our conversation over that long lunch break eventually turned to Mom and Dad's past, as he told me, "Zach, early on in our marriage, if your mom and I hadn't invited the Lord into our lives, we would have likely split up. And then, of course, you and your sister would never have been born. But Jesus changed our lives, and we have done our best to live out our commitment to Him every day." In that moment, I was so glad to be able to say that was the same goal I now had for my own family.

That particular day with Dad, which began like any other workday, became a powerful, pivotal event that forever marked my life. Today, anytime I tell him something that God has done with my music or some new door that has been opened to me, he just smiles and says, "Son, I'm not surprised." Whenever I deal with a tough, challenging, exhausting situation, I recall our conversation as my inspiration and fuel to keep pressing forward into what God is doing. Like Dad said, our heavenly Father is faithful.

Sometime later, after Dad saw my path was going one hundred percent into music and ministry, he told me that the last two years we worked together were some of the best of his life. Those were such amazing and redemptive days for us. With Christ as our bond, we suddenly had so much to talk about and a lot to catch up on. We realized we had more in common than we ever knew, including music. Because God had used a Christian song to get my attention and because of being plugged in at church, I had started listening to gospel music again.

Even before I was old enough to go to work with Dad, I remember hearing Christian music on his radio. Those songs became part of my DNA. They were foundational to who I am. When I began to lead worship, I already knew many classic songs from listening to music with Dad for all those years. I didn't have to learn them, because I had heard them my entire life.

After that conversation about the prophecy, I couldn't help but wonder, "How did Dad keep something like that a secret for thirty-three years? How many times must he have wanted to tell me? Or even to warn me that I needed to stop doing what I was doing so I wouldn't miss out on what God had promised?" But I knew if Dad had spoken too soon, my life might not have worked out the way it did. He waited until he had a peace that my transformation was real. He was patient, letting God work things out with me. He let things play out in the Heavenly Father's timing instead of his own timing.

Crystal's first real experience of unconditional love came through my parents. She once told me, "Everybody else could see that you needed your butt kicked, but your parents just constantly loved you. I couldn't understand why they were treating you the way they did. But then one day, it just clicked—this is what God does, this is who God is. This is grace."

Up until I started working on this book, I had told the story of the pastor's prophecy only a handful of times, certainly not publicly. I had never shared the story in an interview. Honestly, it's hard to talk about without weeping. The whole experience is so humbling because it's not really about me at all. It's about Jesus.

One night before a show at a meet-and-greet dinner with about fifty people gathered around the table, someone on my team asked, "Hey, Zach, will you tell that story about your dad?" I looked up and said, "Now, why are you asking me that? You know how hard that is for me to share." But I agreed, told the story, and ended up crying in front of everyone. All I can think about is the hell I put my family through for all those years while they believed there was something better for me. Yet that is part of the consequences for any of us from the years when we've said no to God.

But something about knowing I was going to tell my entire story with the world prompted me to share the prophecy with the folks who come to my shows. I realized God could use my story to encourage others that God has a plan for each of us and wants to free us to live our lives through His life.

I know God honored my parents through all those desolate and discouraging years because they faithfully prayed for me. I've watched them both walk the walk for a long time. I've seen Christ in them as they've ministered to many people. Had I not watched them live their lives and the way they treat others, I wouldn't be where I am today.

REALIZATION OF REDEMPTION

Today, I have to believe there was a reason why I went down the path I did and lived the life I lived. As I said before, when we turn our lives over to God, nothing is wasted. Even my art degree has come in handy in designing album covers, posters, and merchandise. It's helped me with branding and knowing who I am as an artist and what my lane is. In fact, everything from my past is being used somehow.

As I reflect on the painful events of my life, beginning in my high school days with the basketball coach, I can see how God used even him. Those years created and instilled in me a high level of commitment and work ethic. At that time, I knew if my goal was to play in the NBA, I needed discipline from somebody who wouldn't cut me any slack. I had figured out how to get away with far too much with my parents, but that coach didn't let me off the hook with anything, ever. That's also one of the reasons I butted heads with him so often. He constantly told us, "No, you're gonna do it *my* way!" I came to realize that constant friction and tension helped shape me into the man who God ultimately wanted me to become.

Hebrews 12:7–8 says, "Endure hardship as discipline; God is treating you as his children. For what children are not disciplined by their father? If you are not disciplined—and everyone undergoes discipline—then you are not legitimate, not true sons and daughters at all" (NIV). Discipline *is* always hard at the time, but then you can look back and see how God used a difficult circumstance in your life to change you. Even during high school, those truths were already becoming a part of me.

The most competitive thing I've experienced in music wasn't anything like what I had to deal with while playing basketball. I had to learn how to take criticism from my coaches. That taught me how hard I had to work to be good at something. In the music business, I've seen a lot of creative people struggle with criticism because the artistic, sensitive side of them hears only some kind of rejection. But I see criticism as just another form of coaching that I can learn from. If somebody I respect tells me that something I wrote is not good or not quite there yet, then I'm going to do whatever I need to do to make it better, to get it right. Another big difference in sports and music is in sports you don't ever feel like you've arrived. You don't, you can't, become Michael Jordan. But in music, everybody seems to think you *can* arrive if you just put in the work.

I always feel like my *next* song is going to be my *best* song. And my next song is usually my favorite song too. But then that all changes on the very next album. Why? Because I never feel like I've arrived. It's always funny to hear of someone "discovering" me and automatically assuming I'm some overnight success. They don't know and can't see the twenty-year grind I went through, especially all the hours I put into writing songs and developing my craft before I even wanted to share it with people. I spent ten years alone in my bedroom writing songs before anyone ever heard my music.

Even though Dad was a singer and musician for many years, he never tried writing songs. In fact, he'll hear one of mine and say, "Son, I don't know how you do that. Where do you get that? I always just played other people's songs." But I have much more fun playing a song I've written than performing covers. There is something gratifying about sharing your heart in a song and having people give you instant feedback like, "Man, that's really good." I think that comes from God creating the earth and everything in it over the six days, standing back, and saying, "It is good." Joining Him in that process and response is a gift He will give us when we create.

I'm grateful for the many experiences I've had in my life from sports to working with Dad to making music that shaped and prepared me for my calling. Anytime the subject of work ethic comes up, Dad and I have an ongoing joke: "I'm going to work 'til lunchtime on the day of my funeral."

People often ask me how I feel about finding success much later than most artists, and I am convinced that the reason God didn't allow me to get a record deal until I was on the doorstep of forty years old is that if I had gotten one at a younger age, I would probably have destroyed myself. My heart had to be right and my head on straight for me to be able to handle any level of success. I doubt I would have survived navigating fame in mainstream music, like many young artists who mix "celebrity" with money only to find self-destruction. Today, I can look back and see the purpose in how and why and when everything came together with my music. When my first songs were successful, that was the first time I allowed myself to think, "Okay, this is real. This is something God spoke over my life as a child, and now He's making it happen."

I'll never forget the day that Crystal and I sat down in Nashville with my new manager and entertainment attorney. They were working hard to be realistic with us about the kind of money I might make as an artist. The lawyer told us, "It's going to be a hard grind if you're going to step away from your full-time position at the church. So there's some things you need to know." They had both "been there, done that," so they were warning us not to get too excited or our hopes too high. They cautioned us about the long road ahead. After their speech was over, Crystal told them, "I don't think you understand. God's got His hand on all this, and it's going to work." She had witnessed God's work in our lives and experienced every step of the way with me and could see through eyes of faith where He was taking us.

Even though Crystal and I do walk in faith, one of the biggest misconceptions people have about Christian artists is that our lives are perfect and God has somehow made us into super-Christians. That's not at all true. One of the hardest parts of being an artist is knowing that people put me up on a pedestal. A lot of folks seem to just assume because you're standing on a stage that you must have life figured out. But we fight our daily battles between the good days and bad days, just like everyone else. In fact, when you decide to proclaim God's truth all over the world, the Enemy often comes after you with a much greater vengeance. When you stand up for what you believe and speak to large crowds about Jesus, there is a massive target on your back.

In what I share each night and in the songs I write, I work hard to communicate that I'm just a normal man who's a sinner but serves a big God. My life and my family are far from perfect. Our lives are as messy as anyone's. Occasionally, someone will tell me that one of my songs saved them. I'm always quick to say, "No, a song can never save. I can never save anyone. In fact, I need rescue *every* single day. The only Savior we have is Jesus. My calling may be different than yours, but I have to constantly rely on the grace of God to make it through."

For my mission in music, I'm always going to talk about Jesus, but some of my songs can cross over to other genres, bringing my music to a world of people who may never listen to gospel music. Many Christian artists end up just preaching to the choir and giving the choir what they want to hear. I have a desire to go past that and make sure the gospel is heard by those who may never hear the message any other way. Much like a missionary does.

In Charlie Daniels's memoir, he wrote about going overseas to perform for the troops. He said he would sometimes stay until two or three in the morning talking with soldiers. He had the attitude that these people had given him the lifestyle he's been able to live, so why would he not give them their one moment with him? That's the type of artist, the kind of person I want to be too. I never want to be the guy who says, "Sorry, I can't talk," as I'm rushing somewhere. If it takes me an hour to get to the bus because I need to stop and talk to people, then I will. Because there will come a day when nobody cares who Zach Williams is. I know that. So I want to be in the moment. Because *this* is always the moment, right?

Realizing who my crowd is didn't take me long. Every night, I see big burly dudes with beards in overalls and also a lot of bikers. I can draw some rough people, but that's who I'm trying to reach. If they're coming to my shows, then I'm doing something right. That's why I'm always conscious of and intentional about the songs I write and how we put together the set list at our shows. I know a lot of people who will show up aren't Christians. They're just fans of the music. So I know that every night I need to share my personal story and give some sort of invitation. I need to offer up the gospel. I never want to waste the opportunity I've been given with who I've drawn in the door with my music.

The Beauty of Brokenness

I do so many things wrong that I sometimes have a hard time understanding how God can forgive me so easily. When I willfully disobey Him, when I fail and mess up, I wonder, "How

does He let that go?" Once you truly understand the nature
of sin, you can feel like you're abusing His grace. Crystal and I
talk about that all the time and constantly ask, "Why did God
choose to use me for this? Why did He pick me out of everyone
for this calling? It doesn't make sense for Him to say, 'I'm going
to work through you to write these songs and sing to people.'"
There's no real explanation for it, other than that's just how
God works. And I realize what a huge responsibility I have.

God can use any of us best when we remain in the
mysterious balance of living out our healing, while remembering
our brokenness. Coming out of my past, I don't want to forget
where I've been. That helps keep me humble, because I never
want to go back to my old life. That's also why I write songs from
that same broken place. I want God to take that brokenness
and use it for His good. His grace will always be hard for us to
fully understand, especially when we remember that we don't
deserve it.

It is so cool anytime I get to see someone grasp the gospel
for the first time or come to realize that there's a place where
nobody cares what they've done or where they've been. That's
special to watch because I've had grace extended to me and
know that feeling all too well.

I love that God knew who I was when He made me. He
knew what I would struggle with. He knew about my dad and
our bloodline. That's why Jesus went to the cross for us. He
didn't have to, but He did because He loves us so much even
though we all mess up and fail. That's the very definition
of grace. If we treated everyone with that same attitude,

especially as Christians, the world would be a much better place. Understanding all of that makes me more grateful for what Jesus has done for me.

I am also eternally grateful to the people who point me to Jesus, like my parents, who planted those seeds at an early age. When you've struggled as long as I did, you appreciate everything much more. I would never have been able to do any of the things I have accomplished without God working through the people He's placed around me. Today, I believe that's the only thing rearview mirrors are good for—looking back to be grateful.

When we read the stories of Moses, David, and Paul in the Bible and see that they each had massive moral failures at some point, we discover that God has always worked through people who thought He couldn't possibly work through them. And then in the Gospels we see that the worst people Jesus had to deal with were the religious leaders.

Another connection from my past to my faith is realizing that most addicts, or substance abusers like I was, spend the rest of their lives chasing that first-time feeling. That's why I kept coming back to doing everything I did. I was always trying to put myself back in those first few experiences that felt so good, working to re-create something I never could. But it will never be as fun as the first couple of times. Every time I thought would be *that* time, and it never was.

I've found the same thing can happen in our spiritual lives. When we first come to know that Jesus has set us free, the fire and the "high" we experience can be huge. But we have to be careful that we don't start pursuing that feeling instead of Him. We will all struggle and hit those lukewarm spots in our faith, when we feel like we're just walking through life and not really in the midst of God's will, especially early on, if we're trying to land on our calling or purpose. We have to go past that original feeling to experience what God has next for us. That commitment to press forward can bring maturity and growth. Any of us can go to a hyped-up worship service and get our endorphin levels up. We can work to artificially replicate the feeling of being "spiritual." But taking the next step of obedience in faith isn't always going to *feel* good, but, ultimately, it will *be* good.

THE GOSPEL ACCORDING TO ZACH

Many folks hear my story and then come up to me and say, "I don't really have a testimony like you. I just came to Jesus early in life and have been walking with Him ever since." I always tell those folks, "No, yours is the best kind of testimony! You didn't have to walk through anything hard to realize your need for Him." If that is your story, thank God that you have such a powerful testimony of realizing who Jesus is so early in life. He can use you to reach people no one else can.

Today, for all those who have yet to find an answer, with the internet and social media, the world is full of preachers, loudly offering up all kinds of "gospels" and "truth." Whatever you want, you can find out there. But when you hand your mess of a life over to God like I did, He can take all the broken pieces and put together something you never dreamed possible. The interesting thing is that He won't do that unless you give it *all* to Him. Yet once you begin to see and experience God pulling everything together, life will start to make sense, often for the first time. You begin to understand why He has allowed certain things in your life and what He can do.

The power of the gospel allows me to believe that God's always got me in His arms. Even on my toughest days, even on the days I don't "feel" Him, I know He will keep working in and through me to reach people. I don't understand why He keeps blessing me and why He's so good to me, but He is. I certainly don't feel deserving of all He does. Crystal always tells me, "God just chose you to do this. That's enough." That's why when I see the blessings, I always know it's Him, not me. I spent too many years living the lie that "I'm the man" and it's all about me. Today, my life is all about Jesus.

My past has helped me understand who I am in Christ, to know my message, and to discern who my audience is. I know who God has sent me out to reach. Whether I play in a prison, a church, an arena, or the Grand Ole Opry, I want *everyone* there to love the music but also to be challenged and encouraged about the Lord. I have seen a guy in the front row set down his beer to lift his hands in worship. That's exactly what I'm talking about. I want to reach the people out there who need to know the good news I have found. I feel like God has given me this calling to go out and tell the everyday average Joe and Jane that if Jesus can find and rescue me, then He can do the same for you.

Now, the Christian life makes some things way easier but some things much harder. He will bring a conscience and conviction into your life that you have never experienced before. But you can trust that before you were born, God knew everything you would face. The major difference is that when you accept Jesus, you can stop struggling with the things that have caused you pain for far too long. You can give all of that to Him.

Now that you know my rescue story, I want to be clear that I *never* want to glorify what I did in my past life. I am not proud of *any* of my choices back then. I want this book to be a cautionary tale to anyone who will listen to stay off the road I went down and go straight to Jesus. It's just not worth the heartache for you and your loved ones. And, as we know all too well, far too many people never make it through. I believe the reason God allowed me to survive, the reason He allowed me to live through it all, was so that I can share with you how good He is, how much He loves you, and how much He has and is protecting you even now. The evidence of that fact is you are still alive and reading this.

You might say, "Yeah, but Zach, you just don't understand how bad *my* life is." While I may not have experienced your specific circumstances, I can relate to *anyone* who has ever felt like he or she is a nobody in this world. Out of reach. Invisible. Hopeless. Too far gone. My answer is simply to say, "I get it. I've lived that. Been there. But I'm here to tell you there's a better way to live. He can turn your mess into His message."

After reading my story, you may be realizing for the first

time that God is writing *your* story, right now, in this moment. *Your* rescue story.

I am so grateful today that my past is gone and my present and future are fully in the hands of a mighty God.

And His hands are ready to hold your life too.

All the mistakes, the baggage, the pain—you can give all of you to all of Him.

Rescue is waiting for you, just like it was for me.

And one day, you can look back on your life and say, "There was Jesus."

> *I waited patiently for the LORD to help me,*
>   *and he turned to me and heard my cry.*
> *He lifted me out of the pit of despair,*
>   *out of the mud and the mire.*
> *He set my feet on solid ground*
>   *and steadied me as I walked along.*
> *He has given me a new song to sing,*
>   *a hymn of praise to our God.*
> *Many will see what he has done and be amazed.*
>   *They will put their trust in the LORD.*
>
> —PSALM 40:1–3

AFTERWORD

From Steve and Jenia Williams,

Zach's Parents

Now that you've read our son's story, we're sure you can imagine how very difficult those years were for us as his parents. But through it all, we knew we had to keep choosing to believe God in faith, no matter what we witnessed in Zach's life. We had to have "confidence in what we hope for and assurance about what we do not see" (Hebrews 11:1 NIV).

During Zach's years of struggle, we hung on to the prophecy that the pastor had spoken over him as a baby. We kept thanking God that someday He would bring Zach back to the right path, but there were many difficult days when we said to one another, "How is that ever going to happen?" With no idea how God's word would come to pass, like Luke 2:19 says about Mary, we just "kept all these things in [our] heart and thought about them often."

By his senior year, Zach's rebellion was obvious, even though we didn't yet know that he was smoking pot and drinking, just like his friends. So when he and his two teammates were expelled from school, we were caught off guard and totally shocked. Then, after college, when Zach moved in with the band, living the life of a rock musician, he began to spiral out of control. But that's also when he started writing a lot of original music, with many of his songs ironically having Christian overtones. It was evident in his lyrics that he was searching.

One day, when I (Jenia) was asking God what to do, it came to me that I had to back off from saying things to Zach about church or other decisions I felt he should make. So I prayed, "Okay, Lord, I have to stop thinking that You can't do this without my help. That's it, I'm putting this completely in your hands." Of course, I knew God didn't need my help, but I think, as parents who love our kids, we sometimes have that attitude, mostly out of desperation for any answer. From there, I stopped saying or doing anything. Steve and I realized there are times you just have to get out of God's way.

God used the trip to Europe to get Zach's attention. Once he was back home and told the guys he was done with the band, we saw that he was serious. We knew what a huge step that was for him. Yet, just like Crystal, we wanted to see real change over time. As he stayed the course, we became overjoyed, excited, and grateful. Eventually, it became evident to everyone that Zach's commitment to Jesus was real.

When I (Steve) finally shared the prophecy with Zach that day on the job site, it was before anything big had happened with his music, so we had no idea what God was about to do. When Zach first came to Christ, he had backed away from music completely. Then we saw his desire and focus change when he got the opportunity to sing at church. Even though he was raised around Christian music, Zach never appeared to have any desire to play it. So when God started giving Zach songs to sing and write, that turnabout was unreal to us. From there, everything came together at a miraculous pace.

Now that we've shared some of our part of Zach's rescue

story, we want to speak to the mom or dad reading this with a son or daughter who doesn't know the Lord or a prodigal far away from home. Or maybe you have a spouse or loved one for whom you struggle to see any way that God could ever get through to him or her. If you have been praying and hoping and hurting, we want to share some encouragement with you:

First, love them. Whatever age he or she may be, remember that we are all sinners who have missed the mark many times. We've all made mistakes, and God loves us through them.

> Love is patient, love is kind. It does not envy, it does not boast, it is not proud. It does not dishonor others, it is not self-seeking, it is not easily angered, it keeps no record of wrongs. Love does not delight in evil but rejoices with the truth. It always protects, always trusts, always hopes, always perseveres. Love never fails. (1 Corinthians 13:4–8 NIV)

Second, pray and keep praying. We would often find Bible promises and use them as our prayers, reminding God of what He has written for His children.

> Never be lacking in zeal, but keep your spiritual fervor, serving the Lord. Be joyful in hope, patient in affliction, faithful in prayer. (Romans 12:11–12 NIV)

Third, never give up! Stay the course. As long as your loved one is still breathing, there is always hope. Try your best to stay positive and speak life over them. Even when things look dark, don't let the devil destroy your faith. God will be faithful to His Word. Look at all the times the people in the Bible messed up yet He loved them anyway. That's why He's our example as the perfect parent, not us.

One day when I (Jenia) was driving to work, I began to think on Ephesians 3:14–19. Later, I wrote it down, writing Zach's name into it, and prayed that over him every morning, thanking God for His truth. We've placed the passage below, showing you where to insert your loved one's name so you can pray specifically:

For this reason I kneel before the Father, from whom every family in heaven and on earth derives its name. I pray that out of his glorious riches he may strengthen [name] with power through his Spirit in [name's] inner being, so that Christ may dwell in [name's] heart through faith. And I pray that [name], being rooted and established in love, may have power, together with all the Lord's holy people, to grasp how wide and long and high and deep is the love of Christ, and to know this love that surpasses knowledge—that [name] may be filled to the measure of all the fullness of God. (NIV)

Over the years, we've had the privilege of seeing Jesus turn many lives around. We've known people we thought God might never reach, but then they turned around and surrendered everything to Him. Besides Zach, our daughter Amy's husband, Toby, is one of those, receiving help through a local ministry that leads men out of addiction. We've seen the

Celebrate Recovery program at our church help countless men and women find their way out of darkness.

What Zach's rescue story has done for us as Christ followers is to confirm over and over again the faithfulness of the Lord. And, just as Zach told you, his music's impact on people is not because of him but because of God working through him. After decades in ministry, we are still in awe of what He can accomplish in the lives of His children who love Him.

We also know that many parents have lost their kids to addiction or experienced other tragedies even though they prayed and believed God like we did. We've often wondered why our story turned out the way it did when so many others have not ended well. If that is your story, I wish we had an answer, but we don't. It's just one of the great mysteries of God that we won't get the answer for on this side of heaven. Meanwhile, we just keep trusting Him.

Zach began his story by talking about our family line, so that's how we'll close. When he was at the church in Arkansas, Zach led worship at the university Bible study. One year, around forty students came to Christ. At the end of the spring semester, Zach and the band played a concert to celebrate. As I (Steve) sat there listening to Zach and thinking about the students who had come to Christ, I thought about my granddad who had been a Baptist preacher for over fifty years. He had passed away before any of our kids were born. I thought about Grandpa Williams in heaven and how proud he must be of his great-grandsons. I thought about the legacy God has given our family in bringing people to the Lord. It was an awesome moment as I reflected on how Jesus has made the difference in our lives—the same difference He can and will make in your story.

All our lives, we've had a front row seat to the goodness of God, and in the end, it is always amazing.

> Let each generation tell its children of your
>   mighty acts;
>   let them proclaim your power.
> I will meditate on your majestic, glorious splendor
>   and your wonderful miracles.
> Your awe-inspiring deeds will be on every tongue;
>   I will proclaim your greatness.
> Everyone will share the story of your wonderful
>   goodness;
>   they will sing with joy about your
>   righteousness.
> —PSALM 145:4–7

NOTES

1. Lyrics from "Rescue Story," from the album *Rescue Story*. Words and music by Zach Williams, Jonathan Smith, Andrew Ripp, and Ethan Hulse. ©2019 Be Essential Songs (BMI) / Anthems of Hope (BMI) / Wisteria Drive (BMI) / Cashagamble Jet Music (BMI) / Songs by Fishbone (BMI) / Adm. at EssentialMusicPublishing.com. All rights reserved. Used by permission.
2. Lyrics from "Plan for Me," from the album *A Hundred Highways*. Words and music by Zach Williams, Jonathan Smith, and Jason Ingram. ©2022 Anthems of Hope (BMI) / Wisteria Drive (BMI) / Be Essential Songs (BMI) / My Magnolia Music (BMI) / Cashagamble Jet Music (BMI) / Adm. at EssentialMusicPublishing. com. All rights reserved. Used by permission.
3. Lyrics from "Heaven, Help Me," from the album *Rescue Story*. Words and music by Zach Williams, Mia Fieldes, and Hank Bentley. ©2019 Anthems of Hope (BMI) / Be Essential Songs (BMI) / Wisteria Drive (BMI) / Upside Down Under (BMI) / Adm. at EssentialMusicPublishing.com / Songs by That Dog Will Hunt (BMI) / Capitol CMG Paragon (BMI) / Adm. at CapitolCMGPublishing.com. All rights reserved. Used by permission.
4. Lyrics from "Lookin' for You," from the album *A Hundred Highways*. Words and music by Zach Williams, Jonathan Smith, and Tony Wood. ©2022 Anthems of Hope (BMI) / Be Essential Songs (BMI) / Cashagamble Jet Music (BMI) (admin at EssentialMusicPublishing.com) / Tony Wood Songs (SESAC) /

CURB Congregation Songs (SESAC) / Adm. by Curb Congregation Songs. All rights reserved. Used by permission.

5. Lyrics from "Song of Deliverance," from the album *Chain Breaker*. Words and music by Zach Williams, Jonathan Smith, and Parker Nohe. ©2016 Hipgnosis Songs Essential (SESAC) / So Essential Tunes (SESAC) / Anthems of Hope (BMI) / Be Essential Songs (BMI) / Wisteria Drive (BMI) / Adm. at EssentialMusicPublishing.com / Hillbilly Science and Research Publishing (BMI) / Trailerparker Music (BMI) / Adm. by Warner-Tamerlane Publishing Corp. All rights reserved. Used by permission.

6. Lyrics from "Fear Is a Liar," from the album *Chain Breaker*. Words and music by Zach Williams, Jonathan Smith, and Jason Ingram. ©2016 Fellow Ships Music (SESAC) / Hickory Bill Doc (SESAC) / Anthems of Hope (BMI) / So Essential Tunes (SESAC) / Be Essential Songs (BMI) / Wisteria Drive (BMI) / Adm. at EssentialMusicPublishing.com. All rights reserved. Used by permission.

7. Lyrics from "Good to Know," from the album *Rescue Story*. Words and music by Zach Williams, Jonathan Smith, and Luke Laird. ©2021 Anthems of Hope (BMI) / Be Essential Songs (BMI) / Wisteria Drive (BMI) / Cashagamble Jet Music (BMI) / Adm. at EssentialMusicPublishing.com / We Are Creative Nation Music (GMR) obo itself and Suzanne James Songs (GMR) / Adm. by Concord Global Music (GMR). All rights reserved. Used by permission.

8. Sharon McGowan, "Bono Advises Musicians to Learn from Adam Clayton's Money Woes and 'Pay Attention to Business,'" Irish Mirror, May 31, 2016, https://www.irishmirror.ie/showbiz/irish-showbiz/bono-advises-musicians-learn-adam-8090098.

9. Lyrics from "Turn It Over," from the album *Rescue Story*. Words and music by Zach Williams, Jason Ingram, and Paul Mabury. ©2021 Anthems of Hope (BMI) / Be Essential Songs (BMI) / Wisteria Drive (BMI) / Fellow Ships Music (SESAC) / So Essential Tunes (SESAC) / Flychild Publishing (SESAC) / Adm. at EssentialMusicPublishing.com. All rights reserved. Used by permission.

10. Lyrics from "Stand Up," from the album *Rescue Story*. Words and music by Zach Williams, Mia Fieldes, and Jonathan Smith. ©2019 Anthems of Hope (BMI) / Wisteria Drive (BMI) / Be Essential Songs (BMI) / Upside Down Under (BMI) / Cashagamble Jet Music (BMI) / Adm. at EssentialMusicPublishing.com. All rights reserved. Used by permission.

11. Lyrics from "Love Is a Battleground," from the album *A Hundred Highways*. Words and music by Zach Williams, Tony Wood, and Michael Farren. ©2022 Be Essential Songs (BMI) / Anthems of Hope (BMI) / Adm. at EssentialMusicPublishing.com / Tony Wood Songs (SESAC) / CURB Congregation Songs (SESAC) / Wolf Brigade Music (SESAC) / Adm. by Curb Congregation Songs. All rights reserved. Used by permission.

12. Lyrics from "Chain Breaker," from the album *Chain Breaker*. Words and music by Zach Williams, Mia Fieldes, and Jonathan Smith. ©2016 Hipgnosis Songs Essential (SESAC) / So Essential Tunes (SESAC) / Be Essential Songs (BMI) / Upside Down Under (BMI) / Anthems of Hope (BMI) / Wisteria Drive (BMI) / Cashagamble Jet Music (BMI) / Adm. at EssentialMusicPublishing.com. All rights reserved. Used by permission.

13. Nate Hertweck, "Zach Willaims Wins Best Contemporary Christian Album, 2018 Grammys," Recording Academy Grammy Awards, January 28, 2018, https://www.grammy.com/news/zach-williams-wins-best-contemporary-christian-album-2018-grammys.

14. Lyrics from "There Was Jesus," from the album *Rescue Story*. Words and music by Zach Williams, Jonathan Smith, and Casey Beathard. ©2019 Anthems of Hope (BMI) / Be Essential Songs (BMI) / Wisteria Drive (BMI) / Cashagamble Jet Music (BMI) / Adm. at EssentialMusicPublishing.com / Little Louder Songs (BMI) / Seven Ring Circus Songs (BMI) / Adm. by Kobalt. All rights reserved. Used by permission.